TOOLS OF

NATIVE

AMERICANS

A Kid's Guide to the History & Culture of the First Americans

BUILD
inventions, tools,
and works of art

MEET
the people whose
culture helped
form our own

15
Hands-On
Activities

EXPLORE
the history of Native
Americans with
hands-on activities

LEARN
how the discoveries
of the First Americans
affect us today

Kim Kavin

nomad press

Nomad Press

A division of Nomad Communications

10 9 8 7 6 5 4 3 2 1

Copyright © 2006 by Nomad Press

All rights reserved.

ISBN: 0-9749344-8-8

Questions regarding the ordering of this book should be addressed to

Independent Publishers Group

814 N. Franklin St.

Chicago, IL 60610

www.ipgbook.com

Nomad Press

2456 Christian St.

White River Junction, VT 05001

www.nomadpress.net

Image Credits

Cover Images: chief on horse: courtesy of Jack Hines; tipi: Dave & Brenda Viers, & White Buffalo Lodges, & Marcy Ellis, Artist; p.21: atlatl: courtesy of National Park Service, www.nps.gov; p.33: copper tools: courtesy of Lee Foster, www.fostertravel.com; p.48: sled: courtesy of BTigerlily@telenet.be; p.48: buffalo: courtesy of www.firstpeople.us; p.51: travois: courtesy of Rose High Bear, rose@wisdomoftheelders.org; p.52: chief on horse: courtesy of Jack Hines; p.59: Mogollon pit house: Arizona State Museum, University of Arizona; p.76: bear: www.firstpeople.us; p.87: Arctic: courtesy of Evert Wesker: www.euronet.nl; p.92: igloo: Copyright 2003-2005 Clayton Yee, www.pbase.com; p.95: sled dogs: ca. 1994 by Isa Boucher (Seppala Kennels, Whitehorse, YT, Canada); p.105: Chief Sitting Bull: wikipedia. org. From the Library of Congress: p.30: baby frame; p.31: canoe scene; p.44: chickee hut; p.50: chief; p.53: party on horseback; p.56: three Indians ("Northwestern University Library/Edward S. Curtis's, "The North American Indian: Photographic Images, 2001"); p.81: whaling crew, and fish rack ("Northwestern University Library/Edward S. Curtis's, The North American Indian: Photographic Images, 2001"); p.99: first Thanksgiving; p.100: settlers. From Classroom Clipart: p.1: Indians; p.35: longhouse; p.62: Aztec city; p.80: longhouse; p.95: seal; p.98: Columbus' fleet; p.102: Trail of Tears; p.104: Battle of Little Big Horn. All other images, unless otherwise noted, from Dover Publications.

CONTENTS

TIMELINE

20,000 BCE–8000 BCE—It is believed that the first Americans arrived in the Americas sometime within this 12,000 year period.

5000 BCE—People in the area that is now called Mexico were growing maize.

3500 BCE—People in Mexico were growing squash, beans, and potatoes, and they had learned to make pottery.

2000 BCE—People in Mexico were using calendars, writing in hieroglyphics, studying the stars, worshiping gods, playing games on stone courts, and making books out of deerskin.

1000 BCE—People in Mexico were building temple pyramids.

400 BCE–1500 CE—The Hohokam culture rose to prominence in the Southwest.

300 BCE–1300 CE—The Mogollon culture rose to prominence in the Rocky Mountains.

100 CE—It is believed that Teotihuacán, an Aztec city, housed as many as 200,000 people at this time.

200 CE—At this time Tikal, a Maya city, spanned 23 miles.

1000 CE—Tikal and Teotihuacán had fallen by this time for unknown reasons.

1300–1400—As many as 500,000 Iroquois and Algonquians lived in the Northeast Woodlands and Great Lakes region during these years. It is believed that this was the height of these civilizations.

1400–1500—European explorers arrived in North America.

1492—European explorer Christopher Columbus made landfall in the Americas and described finding "Indians."

1513—European explorer Juan Ponce de León made landfall in modern-day Florida.

1620—The *Mayflower* landed at Plymouth Rock.

1621—The pilgrims and Native Americans shared a feast that became the basis for Thanksgiving.

1650—About 50,000 Cherokee lived in the Southeast at this time, with as many as 200 villages.

1680—Popé leads the Pueblo Revolt.

1741—Vitus Bering died trying to find a land bridge between Siberia and North America. His ship's crew brought beaver pelts home, beginning a fashion fad that inspired many Europeans to set sail for America's Pacific Northwest.

July 4, 1776—The Declaration of Independence signed, establishing the independence of the original 13 colonies.

1804–1806—Within this two-year span Lewis and Clark made their famous expedition.

1828—*The Cherokee Phoenix*, the first Native American newspaper, was published for the first time.

1829—U.S. President Andrew Jackson declared that there was an "Indian Problem."

1830—Andrew Jackson signed The Indian Removal Act.

1838—Roughly 15,000 Cherokees in Georgia, North Carolina, and Tennessee left their homes and walked the "Trail of Tears" to Oklahoma where they were forced to relocate.

1843–1852—Governor Isaac Stevenson of the Washington Territory negotiated 52 treaties that transferred 157 million acres of land from Native Americans to the United States.

1858–1886—Geronimo, an Apache warrior, led raids against Mexican and U.S. settlements.

1864—Native Americans from California who had survived the influx of hostile white settlers during the gold rush were forced to walk 200 miles and relocate near Fort Sumner in New Mexico.

1876—Sitting Bull and Crazy Horse led an infamous battle against U.S. Lt. Col. George Armstrong Custer: the Battle of Little Bighorn a.k.a. "Custer's Last Stand."

1900—By the start of the century less than a thousand buffalo remained alive in North America. One hundred years earlier there had been an estimated 60 million.

1905—U.S. President Theodore Roosevelt invited Geronimo to participate in a Washington, D.C., parade.

1929—James Ridgley Whiteman found spear points and new evidence of a flourishing Native American culture that had existed thousands of years before the European settlers arrived in "The New World."

1939–1945—During World War II, Navajo Wind Talkers enabled the U.S. military to communicate in codes that baffled German and Japanese code breakers.

1964—The Civil Rights Act restored tribal law on reservations.

1970—President Richard Nixon, in a speech to Congress titled "Special Message on Indian Affairs," called for a new era of self-determination for native peoples.

1978—The American Indian Religious Freedom Act became U.S. law, making native religious practices legal again.

1980—The U.S. Supreme Court ruled that the Sioux Indians were entitled to $17.5 million, plus 5 percent interest per year since 1877, totaling about $106 million, for the taking of the Black Hills against the written promises of the Treaty of Fort Laramie.

1988—The Indian Gaming Regulatory Act allowed reservations to build casinos and offer gaming to the general public.

1996—President Bill Clinton declared that every November shall be National American Indian Heritage Month.

2002—With construction under way on the National Museum of the American Indian in Washington, D.C., 500 Native Americans danced during a nearby two-day powwow attended by 25,000 spectators.

2004—The National Museum of the American Indian opened in Washington, D.C.

2006—Several hundred Native American-owned casinos generate about $20 billion in annual gross revenue.

Pacific Northwest: Haida, Tsimshian, Tlingit, Tillamook, Chinook, Älsé, Coos, Coquille, Nootka, Makah, Chinook, Washo, Wishram. Generally known for fishing techniques including weirs, preserving fish by smoking them, using fish oil for cooking and medicine, hunting whales, trading among tribes, and holding potlatch dinners. The Tlingit were specifically known for creating totem poles.

Arctic: Eskimo, Inuit. Generally known for hunting seals, building igloos, and making soapstone candles.

Great Plains: Cheyenne, Lakota Sioux, Comanche. Generally known for hunting buffalo, using travois, and fishing in bullboats. The Comanche were specifically known for horse breeding and handling.

Woodlands/Great Lakes: Algonquian, Iroquois, Mohawk, Oneida, Onondaga, Cayuga, Seneca. Generally known for planting crops, living in permanent structures as well as wigwams, hunting deer and other migratory animals, using wooden tools, smoking food and storing it in silos, making copper jewelry, and trading wampum. The Iroquois were specifically known for living in longhouses, and the Algonquians were specifically known for creating a language.

Southwest/Mesoamerica: Maya, Aztec, Pima, Papago, Hopi, Navajo, Apache. Generally known for building great cities, using hieroglyphics, developing irrigation systems, living in pueblos, weaving watertight baskets, and farming. The Navajo were specifically known for creating dry paintings.

Southeast: Cherokee, Catawba, Creek, Seminole. Generally known for farming, living in permanent structures and even towns, and wearing face paint. The Cherokee were specifically known for creating a language and a newspaper.

INTRODUCTION

N ative American history has been told in many ways. Some of the early U.S. History books taught that the first people of the Americas were savages. Today, of course, we know this was not at all true. Native Americans were hardworking, clever people who made homes and villages and lived in harmony with the natural world around them. The way they did so, and the tools they used along the way, is a tribute to the human spirit.

Tools of Native Americans explores the history of the first people who ever made their homes on the land we know today as the United

States. It traces their evolution from small groups of people working to make tools out of stones and driftwood into large civilizations with complex tools, including calendars and written and spoken language.

We'll take a look at the first people who came to North America and the routes they may have traveled. We'll see how different tribes adapted their homes, cultures, and methods of survival to their environment so successfully that huge civilizations emerged. While we can't look at the history of every single tribe—there are hundreds and hundreds of them, enough to fill dozens of books—we will learn about certain tribes whose lifestyles, living quarters, and tools offer a good example of survival methods and cultures in different parts of the Americas. We'll meet the Inuit, who developed igloos to survive near the Arctic Circle; the Cherokee, who dominated much of the Southeast and developed a written language that spread across the continent; and the Tlingits, who discovered and reaped the benefits of trade and eventually became middlemen for wares brought from all across the Pacific Northwest.

The story of these and other Native Americans is not just a story of survival, but of ingenuity and adaptation in the face of great challenges. Whether inventing ways to preserve fish without refrigeration, creating houses out of nothing but snow, or training horses to become effective partners in battle, the Native Americans continually forged new ideas that remain a strong influence on people all over the world today.

THE FIRST AMERICANS

How did you get here? Not just to where you are sitting and reading this book right now, but to the town where you live? Were you born here, or did you and your family move here when you were younger? How did you move? Was it in a car, or on a train? Why does your family live in one state instead of another? If your grandparents or great-grandparents started out in another country, how did they move across the ocean or from other parts of North America to get here?

Think about the question again: How did you get here?

Scientists have been working for hundreds of years to try to answer that very question—not just about your family,

Bering Strait
land bridge

Possible routes for
Asia–North America
migration

but about all families. Experts have spent countless hours tracing human history back to before your great-great-great grandparents lived, to the time when the very first people made their way across vast stretches of ocean to the Americas. It wasn't 20, 200, or even 2,000 years ago. The best guess is that it was closer to 10,000 or 20,000 years ago.

There was no United States of America back then. There were only two wild continents, North and South America, separated by the great Atlantic and Pacific Oceans from Europe and Asia, where the first human beings appear to have lived. Somehow, and for some reason, groups of these people **migrated** all the way across the oceans to make new lives for themselves in the Americas. They had no maps or cars, and there were no roads or signs to guide them. Nobody had ever been to the Americas before. Not a single person.

The first people to arrive had only themselves and whatever they could build or make from the natural environment around them. With no seeds to plant, no idea what animals they could hunt, and no idea when the fish would be swimming in the rivers, they had to adapt. They had to learn when it would be summer and when it would be winter, and they had to figure out how to get food and shelter for their families all year round.

These people were the earliest Native Americans, the very first people to live on the North American continent.

POSSIBLE MIGRATION ROUTES

Look at a map of the world today, and you will see that a narrow body of water called the Bering Strait separates Alaska and Russia. North of the Bering Strait is the Arctic Ocean, which is the smallest ocean in the world. Even so, it is nearly one and a half times the size of the United States. To the south of the Bering Strait is the Pacific Ocean, which is the biggest ocean in the world. It separates the West Coast of the United States from Japan, China, and all of Asia. Modern ships can easily cross the Pacific Ocean, but even on a big cruise ship that moves relatively quickly through the water, the journey takes days.

It would have been difficult for the earliest Native Americans

to migrate across either the Arctic or Pacific Ocean. They would have risked freezing to death in the Arctic Ocean, and the Pacific Ocean is enormous. It is hard to believe that people from over 10,000 years ago could have constructed boats that would have provided enough shelter, or would have been sturdy or big enough to make such a difficult journey.

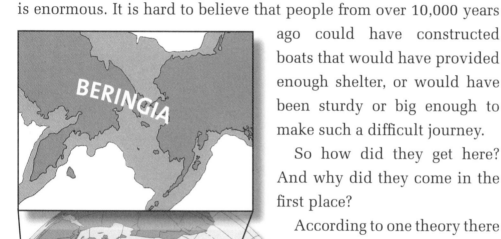

So how did they get here? And why did they come in the first place?

According to one theory there was once an exposed mass of land between Asia and the Americas, south of the Bering Strait, a place that we call **Beringia**. The theory is that Beringia appeared near the end of an Ice Age, when many of the world's oceans were frozen. With all of that seawater bound up in great sheets of ice, land that

Understanding the
Ice Age

Scientists believe that during the Ice Age, much of the world's seawater was frozen into great sheets of ice. This made the oceans shallower, since there was less melted water to fill them up. You can duplicate this phenomenon.

1 Place a scoop of ice cream into your bowl. Notice that when the ice cream is frozen, you can see almost the entire bowl beneath it. During the Ice Age, the ocean floors were exposed in the same way, with all the water frozen on top.

2 Now, let your ice cream melt. Watch how the melted ice cream covers the bottom of your bowl, just like the earth's giant blocks of ice melted to cover the ocean floor. If you had a big enough scoop of ice cream, it would melt enough to fill up the entire bowl, just as the world's seawater has filled up the oceans today.

SUPPLIES

◆ **bowl**

◆ **ice cream**

would have otherwise been underwater was exposed.

Scientists think Beringia was about 1,240 miles from north to south, a little bit longer than California's coastline, and that it was covered in plants and grasses, making it a natural place for animals to graze. In those days, people went where animals went, because animals were a source of food. So, when animals began to cross Beringia from Asia to North America, the earliest Native Americans followed.

> **What is the name of the land-mass that scientists believe was once exposed between Asia and the Americas?**

For some reason, these people decided to stay. Perhaps they liked the new countryside they found. Perhaps the ice sheets began to melt, covering the land bridge behind them. Or perhaps the hunters followed the animals so far south and away from the American coastline that they could not make it back north to cross back into Asia before the season changed to winter.

Evidence suggests there may have been other migrations, too, including people coming by boat from Asia to South America, and others coming from Europe to the East Coast of North America. It is possible, for instance, that these seagoing migrants could have island-hopped by boat across the Pacific Rim, or iceberg-hopped across the Atlantic. However, there is not as much conclusive evidence to support these theories as there is to support the Beringia idea.

Many experts have spent their entire lives studying the

Possible migration routes across the Pacific.

relics that the earliest Native Americans left behind. These relics, many now buried under thousands of years' worth of debris, are the only clues we have as to how the earliest Native Americans got here, and how they lived after they'd arrived.

Create Your Own
Archaeological Site

An archaeological site often contains relics (or items that people from a previous time period used in a given place). These items help archaeologists understand things about their culture and lives. An archaeological site found to contain needles, a loom, dye, some animal skins, and yarn, for instance, was probably where people made clothes. Another site containing a cup, a bowl, and a stick with a scooped end was likely a place where people ate.

The greatest challenge for scientists is to dig up, or excavate, these sites without ruining the relics they contain. Dirt, rainwater, and wind beat down upon the relics over the years, making many of them brittle, or even broken. You can see just how hard it is to be an archaeologist by creating a site of your own.

SUPPLIES

- a few small things to bury
- a place outside to bury things
  - large shovel
  - small trowel
  - spoon
  - soft-bristled brush
  - notebook

FINDING FOOD

Scientists have found evidence of great animals living in the Americas when the first Americans arrived: giant armadillos, mastodons, woolly mammoths, reindeer, saber-toothed tigers, long-horned bison,

1 Collect a few things that you would use for a certain task and bury them in the ground. Say the task is doing your homework. You might bury a pencil, a piece of paper, an eraser, and several paper clips.

2 Dig a wide, shallow hole (several feet and square), scatter some things around, and cover them with dirt. Scatter some more things around and cover them with dirt, too. Let everything you've buried stay there in the sun, wind, rain, or snow for a week or two.

3 Try to dig up your relics, excavating parts of the site with each of the tools listed on the previous page. How easy is it to dig these items up with a shovel? How about a trowel, a spoon, and a soft-bristled brush? Do any of these tools damage the items as you try to unearth them? Your digging process may be slower with a paintbrush that wipes away the dirt bit by bit, but chances are your items are better preserved once they're out of the ground. If you work just with your hands, are you more or less efficient at excavating the site? You'll soon find out just how quickly relics deteriorate, which tools work best for uncovering them, and how challenging it is for scientists to dig them up in one piece.

and more. These creatures were much bigger than the animals that live in the wild today. Beavers, for instance, are thought to have been the size of modern-day grizzly bears. Woolly mammoths weighed three tons and stood 14 feet tall—higher than the average ceiling in a modern-day house. Killing just one of these massive animals could have fed many people for a long time. As a result, the earliest Native Americans, who hadn't yet learned how to grow vegetables to eat, spent a lot of time hunting.

In addition to hunting, it's likely that the earliest Native Americans who lived near the sea collected fish and shellfish, and that those who lived inland dug up and picked wild roots, vegetables, and

HUNTING A WOOLY MAMMOTH

Hunting a 14-foot-tall, wild animal was no easy task for the earliest Native Americans—especially since the only tools they had for hunting were rocks and primitive spears. Yet this is how some of the earliest Native Americans survived, killing the gigantic creatures for meat to eat and skins to turn into clothing and blankets.

Experts believe that the earliest Native Americans hunted these creatures in teams. One hunter would throw a rock at the mammoth's head while several others speared it simultaneously from both sides. With the animal stunned, all the hunters—perhaps a dozen or more—would gang up on the woozy creature and beat it with clubs or rocks until it couldn't fight back. At that point, they would spear its heart, ending the hunt.

In later generations, after the large animals had become extinct, many Native Americans hunted alone or in smaller packs, because they had more efficient hunting tools and went after smaller game.

fruit. Digging up roots (like potatoes, carrots, and radishes) back then was nothing like harvesting them today, because tools were nothing like the shovels and spades in many family's sheds or garages. No, the earliest Native Americans had to make their own tools with whatever they could find. It is likely that they used short sticks with sharp ends to dig up roots, and to pry open clams and other shellfish; and long sticks to help them knock down fruits high up in the trees. There is evidence that they used leaves and tree bark, along with animal skins, to make containers for carrying the food they found.

One of the best tools the earliest Native Americans had was actually their very own hands. Since they had no fingernail files or clippers, they probably had long, sharp nails. Such fingernails would have been an asset in cutting through animal meat as well as the rinds of fruits and vegetables. It is possible that they even used their hands and nails to kill smaller animals, like rabbits.

Perhaps the greatest tool the earliest Native Americans had was their brains. They used their brains to think of and learn how to find enough food for themselves and their families. There were no guns for hunting animals. There were not even bows and arrows at that time. But scientists say they eventually figured out how to make spears with sharp points. This helped them become better hunters, which in turn gave them and their families much more food to eat.

> ## Words to Know
>
> **relic:** item that people from a previous time period used in a given place
>
> **archaeology:** the scientific study of human life and culture of the past, by excavation of ancient cities and artifacts
>
> **carbon-14 testing:** a scientific method for determining an artifact's age based on the amount of carbon 14 element it still contains

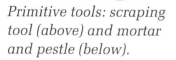

Primitive tools: scraping tool (above) and mortar and pestle (below).

CLOVIS CULTURE

In the 1930s, deep underground in a place called Clovis, New Mexico, scientists found the remains of animals that had been extinct for thousands of years; the experts believe they were relics from a hunting trip that some of the earliest Native Americans took. The animal remains were grouped in such a way that they appeared to have

been slaughtered together all at once, much like how cows are slaughtered today to make steaks and hamburgers.

All around these animal remains scientists found spear points, which were rocks that people had shaped and sharpened. These spear points became known as Clovis points, and prove that the earliest Native Americans made and used tools. The Clovis points, sometimes tied to the ends of long sticks, seem to have been the main hunting tool. Animals that were killed in the hunt would be brought back to the slaughtering area, where they were skinned and cut into separate pieces of meat. The meat was eaten by the tribe, and the skin was probably used as clothing and blankets; it is likely that the bones were turned into tools like scrapers and diggers.

Through carbon-14 testing, relics left behind by the **Clovis culture** were dated back to about 11,200 years ago. This led the world to believe that the Clovis people were the very first people in the Americas. In 1977, however, a new ar-

Carbon-14 Testing

Archaeologists are people who study ancient life and cultures by excavating relics that ancient people have left behind. But when an archaeologist finds something old, say, a wooden spoon, or a spear point made of animal bone, how does he or she know exactly how old it is?

They can tell the age of something through a scientific process called carbon-14 testing. All living things, including trees and animals, absorb a radioactive element called carbon 14, or C-14 for short. It doesn't hurt the trees or animals, in fact, they can't even feel it being absorbed, but it gets into the thing a little bit more every day.

When the living thing dies, the absorbed C-14 starts to break down. The breakdown process is like tiny, microscopic crumbs falling off of a cookie until the cookie is eventually gone. It may take thousands upon thousands of years for that cookie to erode completely, but you can be sure it's crumbling a little bit more every day.

Scientists can measure C-14 so precisely that they are able to tell how old something is based on the rate of C-14 breakdown, A wooden spoon with a moderate amount of C-14 may be hundreds of years old, while a wooden spoon containing only microscopic amounts of C-14 may be thousands of years old.

chaeological site in Monte Verde, Chile, was found. At this site, relics such as tent poles, burned wood, animal hides, and even mastodon meat dated back to 12,500 years ago, making the site 1,300 years older than that in Clovis, New Mexico. Because this site is so much older than the Clovis site, and so far south of where Beringia was, it has also provoked scientists to rethink how the earliest Native Americans got to the Americas. Now it seems just as possible that the Clovis people traveled to the Clovis, New Mexico, area from South America as it is that they came from Beringia.

Where did the name Clovis points originate?

The earliest Native Americans made rocks and bones into tools by banging and sharpening them with rocks. Some of the tools they made were **uniface**, meaning only one side of the rock had been sharpened; others were **biface**, meaning both sides of the rock had been sharpened. Spear points and knives were biface, since banging away at both sides of a rock resulted in a sharper tip. Uniface tools were better for things like scraping animal meat off of bones and for making other tools.

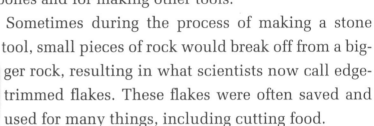

A uniface tool.

Sometimes during the process of making a stone tool, small pieces of rock would break off from a bigger rock, resulting in what scientists now call edge-trimmed flakes. These flakes were often saved and used for many things, including cutting food.

Sometimes rocks were most useful in their natural shapes. Round, smooth stones, for example, were used for hunting. Hunters would throw them at animals,

A biface tool.

either to kill or scare them into running toward other hunters, who would be waiting with spear points. Big rocks with indents were used as grinding stones, like a modern-day mortar and pestle. A person would put seeds or grain into the indented part of a big boulder, and then grind away at it with a smaller, smoother stone to create useful food ingredients, like flour or cornmeal.

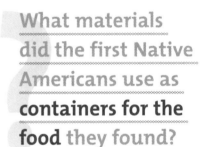

What materials did the first Native Americans use as **containers for the food** they found?

There is some evidence that the earliest Native Americans figured out how to create rope-like cords from tree roots. They would probably use these cords to tie up bundles of freshly picked herbs, to weave into baskets, to hang animal hides out to dry before turning them into blankets and clothing, and to create fishing lines.

THE LIMACE

Not long after the earliest Native Americans learned how to make sharp blades out of rock, they began to create blades of different shapes and sizes for different tasks.

The big blades they made were all very similar to one another—same with all the small blades and thin blades. How did they do this back then? How did they make all the blades within each category so consistent-looking?

The answer is very simple: they would chip away at both sides of a large rock until it was twice the width they wanted their blades to be; then they would split the rock in half by banging the top of it with another rock. The result of this impact would be two, nearly identical blade tools. This type of tool was coined limace, or "slug," by French archaeologists, because when the flat side is placed down, that's what it resembles.

Profile of slug

THE FIRST ART

Most of the earliest Native American tools were designed to help ensure their survival. Life was difficult for these people, and it's likely they spent most of their days looking for food—whether foraging for plants, hunting animals, or trying to catch fish without nets, which hadn't yet been invented. Some experts believe that the earliest Native American artwork came from their need to get excited about upcoming animal hunts, just as you or someone you know might get psyched up before a big soccer game today. Scientists have found paintings on large, smooth rocks and on cave walls that show men with spears chasing creatures like mastodons and saber-toothed

Words to Know

biface tool: a rock or bone tool having two sides chipped for use

uniface tool: a rock or bone tool having one side chipped for use

Clovis culture: the lifestyle of Native Americans who hunted using spear points found at an archaeological site near Clovis, New Mexico

pigment: any coloring matter found in nature

tigers. The paint for these rock "canvases" was made by grinding seeds and roots into **pigment**, which was blended with water and smeared with fingers or primitive brushes. These paintings, which have survived for thousands of years, along with the spear points in places like Clovis, New Mexico, help us understand just how important hunting was to the earliest Native Americans, and how hunters were admired and honored for their bravery and ability to feed the rest of the group.

Indeed, the earliest Native Americans' culture was one of survival, and it left little room for things like song, dance, ceremony, or religion. Imagine if your life consisted of nothing but carrying water from the stream, setting up and breaking down campsites, and digging and picking roots, vegetables, and fruit. This is how life was for the earliest Native Americans—all work and no play.

But that was about to change. New generations of Native Americans, with more complex societies and cultures, were right around the corner.

THE ARCHAIC AND FORMATIVE PERIODS

Something happened around 8000 BCE that would change the lives of Native Americans forever. For some reason, the large animals of the Americas began to die off. The gigantic woolly mammoths, the saber-toothed tigers, the mastodons, and the giant armadillos—they all became **extinct**. Where there had once been countless, massive animals roaming the land, there were none.

Scientists aren't exactly sure why this happened, but the majority of them believe that the melting of the last North American glaciers caused a deadly **climate shift**. According to this theory, significant

8000 BCE

The Great Animal Die-off

5000 BCE
Cultivation of maize by Native Americans

3500 BCE
Shift to agricultural lifestyle and more permanent settlements. Use of pottery

1600 CE
European colonization

← Archaic Period | Formative Period →

changes in temperature killed trees and plants that could not adapt quickly enough to their new environment. With no plants to eat, smaller animals would have died soon afterward. And with no smaller animals to eat, the larger animals would have also died. In short, extinction would have worked its way right up the **food chain**.

Saber-toothed tiger.

Woolly mammoth.

PLANTS AND POTTERY

Scientists have learned that about 3,000 years after the great animal die-off, as early as 5000 BCE, Native Americans in present-day Mexico were growing **maize**, a type of corn. What this discovery means is that sometime after the woolly mammoths and giant beavers became extinct, the Native Americans figured out how to collect corn kernels, plant them, and grow patches or even fields full of corn as a source of food.

About 1,500 years after that, as early as 3500 BCE, squash, beans, and potatoes were also being cultivated. These people had become farmers, at least on a seasonal basis, staying in one place during the growing season rather than only hunting and following their prey.

Astride this change to a more agricultural lifestyle came seasonal settlements, villages, and specific tools that helped Native Americans cultivate and cook the food they grew. Among the most common tools was the manos and the metates,

Words
to Know

extinct: no longer in existence

climate shift: a major change in regional temperature and weather, such as between the Ice Age and the present

food chain: a sequence of organisms in a community in which each member feeds on the one below it

maize: a type of corn

which were used together to grind seeds and corn into meal. Ground meal was mixed with water to form a paste, like pancake batter, which was cooked on a stone griddle, also known as a manioc griddle, heated by fire.

Native Americans were making pottery as early as 3,500 BCE to store the seeds and kernels they ground into meal for future use. They also figured out how to boil plants, roots, and corn inside this pottery. They would heat rocks over a fire until they were as hot as they can be, and then they would move the hot rocks into a pot full of water with a scooper. They would repeat this process, adding more and more hot rocks, until the water was boiling. Why didn't they just hold the pot over the fire? Probably the pots weren't strong enough to withstand an open flame.

The Native American's evolution from the hunting, nomadic life to farming and living in permanent settlements marks the transition between the Archaic and Formative Periods. And it was during the Formative Period that the Native American culture began to flourish in new ways. With more time on their hands, Native Americans of this era became interested in things they'd never imagined when hunting and gathering food was the only priority.

What is the name of the corn that the first Native Americans grew?

FUNERALS AND SPIRITS

Along the Atlantic coast, archaeologists have found the remains of Native American burial grounds containing bodies smeared with red pigment, as if painted during some sort of ritual. Scientists also found ornaments on the graves in which those bodies were found. In other places, such as the Ohio Valley, experts have located vast burial mounds with numerous people, sometimes dozens.

Build an
Archaic Toolkit

The Native Americans who lived during the Archaic Period had to create tools out of things they found in nature. You can do the same thing. Imagine that you have no pots, pans, pencils, knives, or containers. Go out into your backyard or to a local park and gather things you might be able to use as these tools. Remember to think carefully about how you might use every single thing you find. That's what the Native Americans had to do in order to survive.

You might find some sticks that are good for digging and others that are good for spearing. Some rocks are good for hammering and others are good for scraping against other rocks like chalk on a blackboard. You might find leaves that are thick and bushy to stuff pillows, and other leaves that are waxy and strong enough to hold things when they are tied together, like small baskets.

Rocks for pounding or scraping.

See how many Archaic tools you can find near your own house, and then look for more the next time you take a trip somewhere else. You'll see that different areas have different kinds of rocks, sticks, and leaves, and that each of them can be used for different things.

Differnt sticks were used as weapons or for digging or supporting things.

The Atlatl

The Native Americans who lived around 3500 BCE, were not only improving their gardening and cooking skills, but their hunting tools as well. Hunting was no longer the sole focus of their life, but caribou, moose, elk, bears, and other animals roaming North America, made good food, blankets, clothing, and tools. Native Americans hadn't yet invented the bow and arrow, but they had developed the atlatl, which was a type of spear thrower. The atlatl was a thick, hollowed-out stick or bone into which hunters loaded spears. Rather than throwing an entire spear, they would hold onto the atlatl as they whipped the spear at the target. They could "reload" the atlatl with another spear quickly. It allowed hunters to prey upon animals from farther away. Explorers from Europe saw atlatls being used in the 1500s CE in modern-day Mexico, and the tool no doubt existed in the Americas long before that. There is also evidence of it having been used as much as 25,000  years ago in Africa.

Scientists have also discovered mounds and earthworks that they believe were gigantic monuments rather than burial grounds. The Adena people, for instance, who lived in Ohio, Pennsylvania, and southern New York, built a giant, serpent-shaped mound that is five feet tall, twenty feet wide, and a quarter of a mile long. It is just one of more than 11,000 mounds built by the Adena people. Another of them was 68 feet high—that's nearly seven stories tall. Through carbon-14 testing, scientists believe that this work was done around

Words
to Know

atlatl: a thick, hollowed-out stick or bone used as a spear-throwing tool

magnetite: a type of iron ore in which you can sometimes see your reflection

1000 BCE. Imagine how hard it must have been for people to move that much dirt back then, with only their hands and wooden shovels.

Also around 1000 BCE, other Native Americans living far to the south, near Yucatan, Mexico, began to build what scientists call temple pyramids. These people, known as the Olmecs, carved giant, 18-ton heads out of stone and made sculptures of serpents in the same shape as the mound built by the Adena people. These massive sculptures and monuments were religious symbols. The fact that they were so large and took so much thought and effort to construct indicates that communities were becoming permanent.

Further evidence that Native Americans throughout the Americas were shifting from a hunting-for-survival lifestyle into a more stable, permanent-community lifestyle lies in the evolution of their tools. Tools necessary to survive in permanent settlements are different than those needed for hunting and gathering.

How did the first Americans boil water?

A 36,000 pound head carved by the Olmecs.

The relics left behind by the Olmec civilization show that members of this society had specialized jobs. Some were craftspeople, others were farmers, and still others were peasant laborers whose job it was to haul stones for the temples from miles away. This separation of labor could have only occurred in a permanent settlement. Think about it: if they were on the move hunting animals, they wouldn't have had the time or permanent workspace to make whatever type of product it was they specialized in.

The Olmec artisans figured out how to use a shiny material called **magnetite** to create basic mir-

rors which, for the first time, gave Native Americans a way to see their own reflections (beyond looking into a river or stream). It is possible that this discovery contributed to the face-painting and jewelry-wearing trends in this region, since people could now see for themselves how they looked when they decorated their faces and bodies. These trends became so popular that priests and wealthy people even began to have their teeth inlaid with shiny, semiprecious stones.

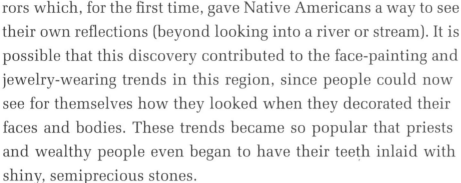

MAYA CIVILIZATION

By about 500 CE, religion and decoration were flourishing in modern-day Mexico, in the Maya civilization. The Maya built a ceremonial city called Tikal (which you'll read more about in chapter 6) at the base of the Yucatan Peninsula. It contained six pyramids, seven temple palaces, several manmade reservoirs, and more. It was a true city in the sense that different people held different jobs and positions.

The Maya traded with other societies for things like honey, cocoa, shells, and cotton cloth. And they began to fashion not only the things they acquired, but themselves, into works of art. They considered crossed eyes to be very beautiful, so mothers often hung beads between their babies' eyes to help pull their pupils inward.

Maya heiroglyphs.

They also admired flat, long foreheads, so mothers would strap boards to their babies' heads, to make their foreheads grow long and slanted. Such things sound strange today, but the Maya would have found us just as odd for dyeing our hair different colors and wearing high-heeled shoes.

There is much evidence that the Maya played games, as did the people of the Hohokam, Mogollon, and Anasazi

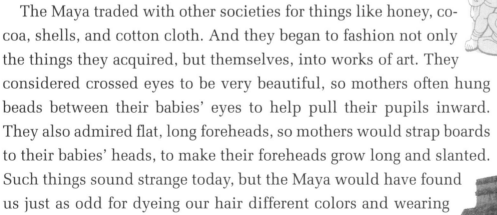

Pyramid at Chichén Itza, Yucaan, Mexico.

Do Your Own
Face Painting

Different kinds of face paint designs gave unique looks for different people. A serious hunter, for instance, would paint black and red stripes across his face, to signify that he was a great warrior. A caring mother, on the other hand, might paint delicate lines in lighter colors on her face, perhaps tracing around shells.

Red was the color of war, and it was usually painted in bands or stripes. White was the color of peace, sometimes painted in a single band and at other times painted in round dots. Black was a "living" color, usually applied to the face in preparation for battle, while a slab of green paint beneath a warrior's eyes was supposed to help him see better at night. Many Native Americans avoided use of the color yellow, as it often signified death.

Try using different colors and designs to make your face look deadly serious with face paint, and then wipe it off and try to make your face look happy and friendly using other colors and designs.

SUPPLIES
- ◆ face paint or face paint crayons
- ◆ a mirror

cultures that followed during the next 1,000 years in New Mexico, Arizona, Colorado, and Utah. The playing of games is a significant development. The earliest Native Americans, who were too busy hunting mastodons to survive, probably never imagined a lifestyle where people would have time to kick a ball around for fun.

We don't know the names of the games played by the Maya, or cultures that followed, but scientists found evidence that games were played. The Maya built sunken courts, 3 feet deep, as game fields where two teams would try to put a rubbery ball through a hoop at the other team's end of the sunken court. The game was like basketball and soccer, but the players could use only their knees, thighs, and buttocks to move the ball. The courts were 132 feet long and 33 feet wide—much smaller than a modern-day soccer field, and about one-third longer, and 15 feet narrower, than a high school basketball court.

What material did the first Americans use to make mirrors?

These early Americans still had to hunt and grow crops to survive, of course, but the improved tools they invented enabled them to accomplish their work faster so that they had a lot of extra time to play games and take part in religious ceremonies. The tribes that emerged from the Anasazi culture in the southwestern United States, for instance, wove huge nets, as big as 240 feet long and 4 feet high, for trapping small animals. This made hunting much easier for them. Instead of having to spend many hours stalking animals with spears, they would string a net across a

The Pyramid of the Sun in Tikal.

large gulley. They would paint a round, black circle in the middle of the net, so that it looked like an escape hole. Rabbits and other small animals would simply run right into it, and the hunters could go home after a short day's work with enough food in hand to feed their families. Members of the Anasazi culture also became so skilled at basket making that their baskets could hold water. That's something that even modern, machine-made baskets often cannot do.

THE CULTURES EVOLVE

All over the Americas, Native American cultures continued to evolve into the cultures that we're most familiar with, those that European explorers like Christopher Columbus and Hernando de Soto would "discover" during the 1400s and 1500s. By the time these explorers began to arrive, there were dozens upon dozens of tribes throughout the continent, each of which had adapted its unique customs and ways of life to its resources and environment. Tribes along the coasts, for example, had become experts at fishing, while tribes further inland were expert hunters. Tribes that lived far to the north had learned how to build igloos of the snow around them, while tribes in the dry desert lands of the Southwest and Mexico were skilled in firing pottery.

It is easiest to understand these cultures and the tools that Native Americans used to build them by exploring different geographic regions of North America. The chapters that follow will explain what life was like in each of the following regions: the Northeast Woodlands and Great Lakes, the Southeast, the Great Plains, the Southwest and Mesoamerica, the Pacific Northwest, and the Arctic.

THE NORTHEAST WOODLAND AND GREAT LAKES TRIBES

THE ALGONQUIAN AND IROQUOIS

When the earliest Native Americans lived between present-day New York City and Detroit, the territory was vast woodland full of trees and animals. It stretched all the way up into New York state and Connecticut, down to New Jersey, Delaware, and Maryland, and west through Pennsylvania to the Ohio Valley. There, it connected with the Great Lakes.

Since the last North American glaciers melted, around 10,000 years ago, the climate in this area has been similar to how it is today, with hot summers, cold winters, and moderate autumns

and springs. Although Native Americans found ways to survive everywhere in the Americas, this region's more moderate temperatures made for more comfortable living than, say, the Arctic Circle. Here, people could make the most of the seasons, growing enough crops and hunting enough game during the spring, summer, and fall to last them through winter. Throughout the ages, the tribes who inhabited this region lived a variety of different lifestyles. Some preferred hunting and migrating with the animals, while others settled in one place and grew crops.

These different lifestyles called for different types of shelter. People who lived in the same place year-round needed to build permanent structures, while those who followed migrating animals needed to live in movable shelters.

Archaeologists have discovered that Native Americans who farmed in the Ohio Valley built circular houses suitable for the climate in all seasons. To build these houses they began by digging circular holes. Next, they lined the circumference of these holes with wooden posts, After lashing these wooden posts together with flexible plant material, they made rooftops out of **thatch** found in the woods. Because these homes were partly underground, and well insulated yet breathable, they made good homes for every season of the year.

East of the Ohio Valley, Native Americans who hunted lived in wigwams, which were temporary shelters that could be moved. They made these structures by placing four or more uprooted **saplings** into the ground and tying their tops together in the center. Next, they covered this frame with long

Roundhouse.

strips of tree bark that were sewn together and insulated the inside with swamp grass. After that they hung an animal skin door, and laid fir tree boughs as carpet.

NEIGHBORING LANGUAGE FAMILIES

The Iroquois was a confederacy of tribes united by a common language, Iroquoian. Iroquois tribes lived all over upper New York state, the St. Lawrence Valley, and the shores of Lakes Erie and Ontario. The Algonquian was a confederacy of tribes as well. They lived west of Iroquois tribes, in the Great Lakes area— and they too were linked by the same language. Historians believe that there were about 500,000 Native Americans in the Eastern Woodlands in the 1300s and 1400s, and most of them were members of one of these two language families.

Wigwam.

The Algonquian language was spoken across all of North America, similar to how English is spoken throughout the United States; and some of the Algonquian words even made their way into the English language. This development of one, widely-spoken language was important, as it gave tribes from different places a way to communicate with one another, just as people today from Texas, Massachusetts, and England are all able to communicate in English.

How do you build a wigwam?

Life for the Algonquian and the Iroquois involved a lot of tools, many of which were made from trees. From just the bark of a tree,

Iroquois pattern of woven moose hair.

Mother with baby in a baby frame.

these Native Americans made house walls, food and water containers, eating trays, canoe skins, and even woven nets. Tree roots were used like rope to tie things together, while the wood of the tree itself was turned into anything from spears and arrows to canoes and snowshoes. Wood was even used to make **baby frames**, into which mothers would strap their babies.

In order to make these tools from trees, Native Americans developed tools for working with trees. When the European explorers came in the 1400s and 1500s they discovered that the Native Americans had axes for cutting trees down, and they had also developed **adzes**, which are like axes but are used to shape pieces of

What kinds of tools did the Iroquois and Algonquians make from trees?

Learn to
Speak Algonquian

Algonquian is not just one language, but a group of related languages. Algonquian was widely spoken in North America before the European explorers arrived. Today, Americans still use about 100 Algonquian words, including the names of certain places provided by Algonquians.

See how many sentences you can put together using these Algonquian terms:

hickory	moccasin	succotash	tomahawk	wigwam
hominy	moose	terrapin	totem	woodchuck

wood. The Native Americans in these parts had also created **gouges**, which are used like modern-day **chisels** for scooping out pieces of wood. Gouges were particularly useful in digging out tree trunks to make canoes.

The Algonquian and Iroquois grew corn, tobacco, and other crops, but they also hunted for food. One type of animal they found in great

Words to Know

baby frame: a wooden board that mothers would strap their babies into; it was hung from a hook to keep babies safely out of the way during chore times

adze: an ax-like tool for trimming and smoothing wood

gouge: a chisel with a curved, hollowed blade, for cutting grooves or holes in wood

chisel: a hand tool with a sharp, often wedge-shaped, blade for cutting or shaping wood and stone

snare: an overhead net attached to a ground-level trigger, designed to entangle animals

quantities in their northern territories was moose, which do not run in herds, and therefore have to be hunted one at a time. Native American hunters in this region invented several tools to lure moose into their traps. From birch bark they created whistle-like instruments that made a sound similar to the moose's mating call. They would use this to lure a moose toward an overhead **snare** hung from tree branches. The snare would fall after the moose stepped onto a connected branch on the ground, trapping the animal until hunters could kill it. In the Great Lakes area, many Native Americans became experts at fishing, too. They learned that some fish were attracted to light, and so they would strap torch lights onto their canoes, paddle out into the lakes at night, and wait with spears for the fish to swim toward the light.

The hunting methods of this period were far more advanced than those of the earliest Native Americans, which meant that the people who lived during these later years could sometimes catch

Hunting from the reeds.

Create Your Own
Algonquian Art

Much of what we know about the Algonquian people comes from pictographs and petroglyphs, two styles of artwork that many Native American tribes produced. Pictographs are paintings done on bark, while petroglyphs are images scratched onto stone.

Today, you can practice both kinds of artwork.

1 To make a pictograph, find a large piece of bark (or use a piece of paper as a substitute) and paint a common scene taken from the world today. For instance, you might create a scene that shows you studying or doing your homework at the kitchen table when you get home from school.

2 To make a petroglyph, find a large rock and use a smaller rock (or a piece of chalk) to scratch out a similar scene. This time you may want to draw yourself playing your favorite sport.

3 When you've completed both the pictograph and the petroglyph, compare them to decide which best captures an image of how Americans live today. Is one more detailed than the other?

SUPPLIES

- a piece of bark (or a sheet of paper)
- paints
- a rock with a flat surface
- a smaller rock (or a piece of chalk)

more food than they actually needed. Because they had no refrigerators or freezers to store a surplus of food, they had to find a way to preserve it.

Archaeologists have discovered evidence that Native Americans of the Eastern Woodlands used smoke to preserve their food and stored it in **silos**, much like the way modern-day farmers store their corn, wheat, and other crops. The Native American silos were deep holes lined with marsh grass and covered with bark to keep out the animals and weather.

The Native Americans who lived in the Eastern Woodlands and Great Lakes regions during the 1300s and 1400s were concerned with their appearance. In the Great Lakes region, people dug up copper and became experts at pounding it into earrings, nose rings, and other forms of jewelry. To make copper jewelry (as well as other copper items like fishhooks, blades, and drills), they would pound a nugget of copper into a thin sheet, like a rolled-out piece of dough. Then they would outline whatever it was they were making in the metal sheet with a sharp point. Next, they would crack the sheet until the outlined item emerged. Scientists have found copper jewelry and other copper items made in this fashion from the Great Lakes to as far as New York state.

The Iroquois are known to have carved hair combs out of animal bones, and some Native Americans used mussel shells found along the Atlantic or Great Lakes shores as tweezers to pluck out unwanted hair. People also used the shells they collected to make jewelry or **wampum**.

Why did the Native Americans hunt moose with single traps?

Copper Native American tools from present-day Michigan.

Wampum from shells.

Wampum bracelet and belt.

The word *wampum* comes from the Narragansett word for "white shell beads." Usually, wampum was either white or purple-black. Different colors and designs of wampum had different meanings. A purple background encased in a white border, for instance, sometimes indicated a once-hostile relationship turned peaceful, and wampum belts that were painted red were a call to war. Native Americans searched the beaches of present-day New Jersey and Long Island for whelk shells, which were the most common shells used for wampum. They would poke holes in these shells and then string them together into long belts that were used as decoration and to tell stories.

What is a silo?

When Europeans arrived in the 1400s and 1500s—many decades after the Native Americans began creating wampum—wampum evolved from a decoration and form of communication into a form of currency. It was more abundant than metal coins, so European explorers began to trade it for goods and services, just as they would have traded coins if they had carried enough of them to pass around in the New World. White wampum was worth half as much as purple-black wampum, as there were far more white shells to be found on the beaches. A six-foot strand of purple-black wampum would fetch about 20 shillings in the 1700s, or about 175 U.S. dollars today, in 2006.

WARRING TRIBES AND IDEAS OF PEACE

What do you use to make wampum?

As the Algonquian and Iroquois tribes grew in health, wealth, and size, they began to bump into one another's campsites, hunt one another's animals, and generally get into one another's way. Some of these people were willing to fight to keep what they believed was their territory.

The Iroquois, thanks in part to their ever-expanding population,

Life in a Longhouse

Iroquois villages consisted of two or more longhouses, which were originally built next to rivers for easy access to water, but later were constructed on hilltops for protection from nomads and other tribes. Longhouses reached up to 150 feet long and housed anywhere from 30 to 60 people. A path ran the length of the longhouse, and curtains hung on either side of the path to allow each family a small amount of privacy. The curtains, like the longhouse door, were made of animal skins, and each private area was no bigger than six by nine feet. That's about the size of a modern-day bathroom—and it was the private area for a mother, a father, and their children. Imagine sleeping in a room that size with five or six people every night!

rose to prominence in the 1300s. Despite their continued dominance in battle, they actually were very friendly societies. They lived in **longhouses** that were sometimes 150 feet long, and they called themselves the Haudenosaunee, or "People of the Longhouses." Each longhouse contained "booths" that families slept in, with curtains hung up for privacy.

The oldest woman was put in charge of the longhouse. Except for the men's hunting tools and clothes, she was considered the owner of everything in it. It made sense for the women to be in charge, since the men were often gone for long periods of time hunting animals. Women oversaw all the daily chores and duties, from food preparation and the sewing of clothing, to making sponges out of corncobs and helping their daughters sew together dolls using **corn silk** for doll's hair.

Words to Know

silo: an airtight pit or tower in which food can be preserved

wampum: seashells strung together into long belts that could be used to convey messages or as currency

longhouse: the traditional sleeping building of the Iroquois, as long as 150 feet, with curtained "booths" for each family

Words to Know

corn silk: the long, silky fibers that hang out of a corn husk; sometimes used to make doll hair for Native American children

tomahawk: a war club on a wooden stick—after the Europeans came to the Americas and introduced metal, a spiked metal ball was often affixed to the top

Over time, the Iroquois came to dominate the Algonquian tribes and all the other Native Americans living between New England and the Mississippi River, from Ontario and Tennessee. They used all the tools they had when they went to war: spears, knives, rocks, and war clubs, or **tomahawks**—wooden sticks with spiked metal balls or ax points on top.

A prophet known as Deganawidah was disturbed by this violence; as the story goes, he had a vision one day of many tribes uniting instead of fighting among themselves. Later, one of his followers, Hiawatha, persuaded five Iroquois-speaking tribes—the Mohawk, Oneida, Onondaga, Cayuga, and Seneca—to come together in a political group known as the Five Nations. Instead of fighting each other they worked together, and when Europeans arrived in North America and began trying to take control of the land they stood together in defiance.

Later, a sixth tribe known as the Tuscarora would join, making it the Six Nations. The French, English, and Americans referred to this group as the Iroquois Confederacy.

Hiawatha

Hiawatha is credited with founding the Five Nations, but he was not always a peaceful man. For a time he lived alone, killing and eating wandering travelers. The story goes that one day while Hiawatha was cooking one of his victims he saw a face in his pot. It was Deganawidah, the spiritual prophet who had originally envisioned the Five Nations. Deganawidah persuaded Hiawatha to stop eating people and to instead eat deer, and Hiawatha promised to atone for all the deaths he had caused by spreading Deganawidah's message of peace. The Five Nations eventually became one of the most powerful groups in North America.

Check out the round, permanent structures that the Cherokee used as homes

Meet Sequoyah, who invented a written language for the Native Americans

Learn about the lifestyles of the Catawba and Creek tribes

CHAPTER
4

THE SOUTHEAST TRIBES

THE CHEROKEE, CATAWBA, CREEKS, AND SEMINOLES

The region that makes up Virginia, the Carolinas, and Georgia is somewhat different from that of the Northeast Woodlands. It is defined by the vast Appalachian Mountain range, which actually starts up north but stretches all the way south to Atlanta, Georgia. Many of the southern Appalachian peaks are between 2,000 and 4,000 feet high, but in North Carolina, Mount Mitchell rises to a whopping 6,684 feet. Many rivers wind their way down the mountainsides to sea level and eventually find their way to the Atlantic Ocean.

The tribes throughout this region developed different kinds of skills, because life in the Appalachian Mountains was different from life along the Atlantic coast. Inland tribes focused on farming while those along the coast became experts at fishing. The temperature ranges within the Appalachian Mountain region were wide, with frigid winter nights on the mountain peaks and sultry summer afternoons just inland of the coast. This also contributed to their development of different life styles and skills.

THE CHEROKEE

Over time, the Cherokee tribe came to dominate much of the Southeast region. There were about 50,000 Cherokees by the mid-1600s, controlling much of the Carolinas, Georgia, and Alabama. They lived in at least 200 villages, some of them stretching into parts of Virginia, Tennessee, and Kentucky.

For the most part, the Cherokees were farmers who stayed in their villages all year round. For this reason, they built strong permanent structures. A typical village had as many as 60 circular houses that were built out of tree branches shaped to look like an upside-down basket. Each house was built on a large, round hole that was dug into the ground, similar to how cement foundations are built into the ground for houses today. Like the circular houses of the Algonquian, the earth kept the inhabitants warm during the winter and cool during the summer. It was a comfortable place to sleep, and the dirt floor was a perfect, non-flammable place to build a fire for cooking food.

Cherokee symbol of the Sun Myth.

To further insulate their homes, the Cherokees spread a layer of mud over the branches that formed their aboveg-

How many **Cherokee** people lived in the Southeast around 1650?

round walls and roofs, in a technique called wattle and daub, with the wattle being the branches and the daub being the mud. Eventually, thick logs replaced thin branches used in construction. These made the dwellings stronger, and the Cherokee homes began to look more like log cabins than thatched huts. Rather than using mud to cover the log walls entirely, it was used only to fill in the cracks between logs.

Cherokee council house.

Each home had a single doorway, plus a hole in the roof to let smoke escape when a fire was burning inside to cook food or generate heat. In many ways these log structures were like the log cabins people build today, only now we have brick or stone fireplaces connected to chimneys instead of just smoke holes in our roofs.

Since the Cherokees lived in permanent settlements, it made sense for them to create what we might today call a "downtown" area—a

COUNCIL HOUSE TRADITION

Most communities today have at least one building that serves the same purpose as the Cherokee's council houses: bringing people together. Your town hall, for example, is a gathering place where adults decide what roads and streetlights the community needs to build. Your post office is a gathering place where adults and children buy stamps and send letters to friends and relatives. And your school is a gathering place where children are taught the ways of the town, state, nation, and world.

Imagine how different your community would look, act, and feel if you did not have places like schools, post offices, or town halls? How would you know who your neighbors were? Or what they cared about? Or when they needed help?

Try to list at least 10 other buildings in your community where people come together and strengthen your society.

place for the villagers to get together and discuss matters of importance to the whole community. These meeting places were called council houses. To add prominence to these structures, they were sometimes built atop hills or dirt mounds. Inside, people would hold religious ceremonies, general meetings, and gatherings of important leaders.

Sequoyah's "Talking Leaves"

Perhaps the most famous Cherokee was a man named Sequoyah, who invented a written language. Sequoyah never received a formal education, but he did learn to speak several Native American languages. He also recognized that people who could read and write instructions or information had an advantage over those who could only communicate face-to-face through speech.

Sequoyah felt that his people needed to have a written language to unify them. A written language would help them coordinate their attempts to stand up to Europeans pushing into their land. Ironically, the name *Cherokee* is a form of a word that means "people of a different speech."

After many years of thought, Sequoyah came up with the idea for what he called "talking leaves." He had been part of a meeting with white settlers who ventured into the Cherokee lands during the late

Sequoyah's "Talking Leaves."

1 A, short. 2 A broad. 3 Lah. 4 Tsee. 5 Nah. 6 Weeh. 7 Weh. 8 Leeh. 9 Neh. 10 Mooh. 11 Keeh 12 Yeeh. 13 Seeh. 14 Clanh. 15 Ah. 16 Luh. 17 Leh. 18 Hah. 19 Woh. 20 Cloh. 21 Tah. 22 Yahn. 23 Lahn. 24 Hee. 25 Ss (sibilant.) 26 Yoh. Un (French.) 28 Hoo. 29 Goh. 30 Tsoo. 31 Maugh. 32 Seh. 33 Saugh. 34 Cleegh. 35 Queegh. 36 Quegh. 37 Sah. 38 Quah. 39 Gnaugh (nasal.) 40 Kaah. 41 Tsahn 42 Sahn. 43 Neeh. 44 Kah. 45 Taugh. 46 Keh. 47 Taah. 48 Khan. 49 Weeh. 50 Eeh. 51 Ooh. 52 Yeh. 53 Un. 54 Tun. 55 Kooh. 56 Tsoh. 57 Quoh. 58 Noo. 59 Na. 60 Loh. 61. Yu. 62 Tseh. 63 Tee. 64 Wahn. 65 Tooh. 66 Teh. 67 Tsah. 68 Un. 69 Neh. 70 ——— 71 Tsooh. 72 Mah. 73 Clooh. 74 Haah. 75 Hah. 76 Meeh. 77 Clah. 78 Yah. 79 Wah. 80 Teeh. 81 Clegh. 82 Naa. 83 Quh. 84 Clah. 85 Maah 86 Quhn.

1700s. The white people did not always stand by their words, so to Sequoyah those words seemed like leaves that simply blew away in the wind. He felt the Cherokee should have their own talking leaves

The Cherokee Phoenix

In February 1828, after Sequoyah's "talking leaves" had become widely understood throughout the Cherokee Nation, the first Native American newspaper was published. It was called the *Cherokee Phoenix*.

The creation of the *Cherokee Phoenix* was an important hallmark in Native American history. It was the first time that the day-to-day viewpoint of Native Americans was written down. Reading the same newspaper gave Cherokees throughout the Southeast a sense that they were part of a much greater group, a nation unto themselves. It helped educate them about what was happening to people in other Cherokee villages as Europeans continued to come ashore and the United States continued to expand westward.

Although other Native American tribes did not speak the Cherokee language, the newspaper's editor soon realized that these tribes had many of the same interests and concerns as the Cherokee. And so, in 1829, the name of the newspaper changed to the *Cherokee Phoenix and Indian Advocate*.

The newspaper continued to run articles that explained and defended the rights of Native Americans until 1834, when it ran out of money, partly because the U.S. government refused to pay debts it owed the Cherokee people. For a year the paper went unpublished despite attempts to start it up again, until it was closed down permanently when the press was destroyed in a raid.

that would be more meaningful to them, so he invented 86 characters, or sounds, to form an alphabet. Within a few years, almost everyone in the entire Cherokee Nation understood how to communicate using the alphabet.

Words
to Know

literate, literacy: the ability to read and write

For the first time, a group of Native Americans became **literate**. They used language as a tool to spread information and record history in a way that no group of Native Americans had done in the Americas. Up to this time, Native Americans used only pictures and verbal stories to pass on their heritage and help their individual cultures grow. Now, with a written language, the Cherokee could communicate their message on a much wider scale and document their societies forever.

Why did the Cherokees make part of their homes underground?

CATAWBA AND CREEKS

Creek pattern.

The Cherokees were the biggest tribe in the Southeast, but they were not the only one. There were also the Catawba and the Creeks, as well as the Chickasaws, Shawnees, and Choctaws. As the Cherokee Nation grew and spread throughout the Southeast, it fought with the Catawba and the Creeks, particularly in the mid-1700s. After several years of fighting, the Cherokee forced the Catawba and Creeks farther inland and out of their way.

Catawba is a word that means "river people," an appropriate name as that tribe lived along the Catawba River in the Carolinas. The Catawba were fierce warriors who believed in looking as imposing as they acted. They used face paint to frighten their enemies, painting a black circle around one eye, a white circle around the other, and the rest of their face black. They also used boards to flatten the foreheads of baby boys, a tradition that made the adult warriors' face paint stand out even more.

Another confederacy of tribes that fought against the Cherokees was the Creeks. Like the Cherokees, the Creeks had permanent towns, which they called *italwa*. They also had smaller communities nearby that they called *talofa*. These communities would be formed whenever a main town had about 500 people in it. Their purpose was to spread the Creek way of life and keep the *italwa* from becoming over-populated. Members of the Creeks would often travel to italwas and talofas other than their own to visit and stay connected with family and friends.

By the end of the 1700s, the women of the Creeks were using plows and axes, as well as raising livestock. Some of their homes were separated by a solid mile of corn, rice, or potatoes. Remember, they had no machines or tractors with which to till and plant the soil. They had to tend all those crops by hand, an incredibly difficult task with no modern tools.

A Creek woman farming.

Because the Creeks' spread-out lifestyle required a lot of land, their society began to clash with the Cherokee society. Both societies were growing, and there was not always enough land for hunting between their settlements. Unfortunately for the Creeks and Catawba, there were simply too many Cherokees for them to overcome. The Cherokee came to dominate the area, until the 1800s when the United States of America began removing the Cherokees and giving their land to white settlers. (You'll read more about this in chapter 9.)

Who invented the Cherokee written language that spread across the United States?

THE SEMINOLES

Another Southeastern tribe whose name is widely known today is the Seminoles. "Seminoles" are the mascot for Florida State University, whose students paint their faces before important sporting events, similar to how Native Americans did before battle. Some descendants of Native Americans are upset by this tradition, because they feel it makes a mockery of their ancestors. As a result of these concerns, many American universities and colleges are changing their mascots.

It is ironic that Florida State University has embraced the Seminoles as their mascot for battle on the athletic fields, because the real Seminoles were peaceful people by nature. They were descendants of the Creeks who moved south to avoid fighting with Cherokee tribes and U.S. troops, and to take advantage of vacant land in northern Florida. Eventually the Seminoles retreated to Florida's swamps where they were left alone, for the land had little value to farmers and was therefore not worth fighting over. To survive in the swamps, the Seminoles created chickee huts, which were thatched huts that could be constructed in a single day. *Chickee* means "house" in the Seminole language. Chickee huts had floors of dirt or, in places where the earth was very soft, of split logs.

What was the purpose of Cherokee council houses?

The name Seminole actually means "wild people" or "runaway," though in this case, running away or retreating was a tool of survival. If the people had stayed where all the fighting raged in the Carolinas and Georgia between the Native Americans and the white settlers, they likely would have been killed. Moving south helped them to preserve their culture, which continues today.

A thatched chickee hut.

CHAPTER 5

THE GREAT PLAINS TRIBES

THE CHEYENNE, LAKOTA SIOUX, AND COMANCHE

The Great Plains of North America stretches far and wide, from Canada all the way south through the Dakotas, Nebraska, Kansas, Oklahoma, and Northern Texas. It covers the land as far west as the Rocky Mountains. This is a wide-open space filled with different kinds of grasses that can live without a lot of rain.

As you might guess, the dry, grassy land didn't always make for easy farming for the Native Americans who lived there, but it did make for excellent grazing for herd upon herd of buffalo. Buffalo was the main source of food for the people of this region, and so they moved with the buffalo, hunting them along the way.

GREAT PLAINS REGION

Lakota woman using a travois.

It's not easy packing up your house and belongings every couple of months, but the Native Americans in this part of the continent invented tools that would help to make this process easier. The Cheyenne and Lakota Sioux tribes used **travois**, or sleds, pulled by dogs to move their belongings. *Travois* were made of two long poles connected with material that was almost like a net. One end of each pole was attached to the dog's shoulders, and the other end simply dragged on the ground behind the dog as it walked. Native Americans would load the net-like material between the poles with supplies, which the dogs would pull across the Plains.

The *travois* was a smart tool, not just because it made moving easier but because it could be taken apart and used for other things once the tribe arrived at its new camp. The long poles that made up the travois were used to build fences to trap buffalo. The poles were also used to create frames for shelters, like **tepees**. Indeed, the poles were excellent multipurpose tools.

Words to Know

travois: a sled consisting of a net or platform dragged along the ground on two poles that are pulled by a horse or dog

tepee: a cone-shaped tent of animal skins or bark

moccasin: a shoe made of soft, flexible leather or animal skin

THE ALL-IMPORTANT BUFFALO

It was important for the people of the Great Plains to have tools that they could carry with them and use again and again. Because they had to continually track buffalo herds, they didn't have much time to make new tools. When they did make new tools, they made them out of buffalo remains.

They used buffalo hides for making cradles for newborn babies, curtains, tepee walls, clothing, and blankets. Sometimes they would even stretch a hide until it was taut and use it as a canvas for painting pictures. Buffalo tails were excellent

What is a travois?

Create Your Own
Rattle

Native American children did not have many toys and those they had were made from things that they and their parents found in nature. One of the more common toys was a rattle made from the hoof and skin of a buffalo. You can make a similar rattle using a cow's hoof.

1 Cut your piece of cloth into a large square that can be wrapped around the entire cow's hoof. Cut a second piece of cloth into a strip about 2 feet long.

2 Fill the open side of the cow's hoof halfway with uncooked rice, and then wrap the cloth tightly around it. Use the 2-foot strip of cloth to tie off the ends of the bigger piece of cloth, securing it as tightly as possible. You want the big piece of cloth to be taut, so the rice will bounce off of it the same way it bounces off the insides of the cow's hoof.

SUPPLIES

- a piece of cloth (the thicker the cloth, the more it will resemble the buffalo hide that Native Americans used)
- some uncooked rice
- a cow's hoof (you can find these in the dog treat section of any local pet store)

flyswatters. Buffalo hair could be woven into rope, as well as used for stuffing pillows, **moccasins**, and gloves. These Native Americans carved buffalo horns and bones into spoons, cups, knives, and awls (a puncturing tool). They used the largest bones of the buffalo, like the ribs, to create small sleds. They even made use of buffalo hooves, turning them into rattles for children.

A child's sled made from buffalo ribs.

FISHING IN BULLBOATS

When some of the Native Americans living in the upper Missouri River area weren't hunting buffalo, they fished in one of the many rivers that wind through the Plains. Some of these rivers, like the Missouri and Knife Rivers, are so big that the Native Americans needed boats to cross them. What do you think they used for making boats instead of trees? That's right: buffalo.

The frame of the boat they made, called a **bull-boat**, was made of willow branches tied together

What are some of the things Native Americans could make out of buffalo?

Build Your Own
Miniature Bullboat

1 First, you'll need to build your bullboat's hull. Take a piece of aluminum foil and place a bowl in its center. Wrap the foil up the sides of the bowl, and then remove the bowl. You'll have a hollow, rounded hull, the shape of a Native American bullboat.

2 Now, try to make your boat go in a straight line across a bathtub or sink full of water by blowing on it. You may be able to make it go straight, but the boat will probably spin in circles. Imagine how dizzy you'd become if you were sitting in that boat.

3 To get your boat to travel in a straight line without spinning in circles, you'll need to add a rudder, like the Native Americans of the Great Plains did. You can do this by taping or stapling a piece of a Popsicle stick to one side of your hull. Try different lengths of Popsicle sticks until you get it right.

SUPPLIES
- aluminum foil
- a bowl
- Popsicle sticks
- tape or a stapler

with buffalo hair. These boats were shaped like a saucer. Buffalo hide stretched over the frame served as the boat's hull. People sat in the hull and paddled with large sticks or with their hands.

To steer this saucer-shaped boat, the Native Americans attached

What is a bullboat?

a piece of wood to the buffalo tail which they dropped into the water and used as a rudder.

HORSES AND COMBAT

When Europeans began to explore the Americas, they brought horses. Nobody is sure when the first horses arrived or on which ship they came, but it is believed that horses had arrived in the Americas by the 1500s. Some of these horses

Make Your Own
War Bonnet

When preparing for battle, some Native American warriors in the Great Plains would put on war bonnets. Each bonnet consisted of a headband with feathers sticking out of its top, with the most important feathers in the front, right above the warrior's forehead. Other feathers were tied to the sides of the headband, so that they hung down around the warrior's neck and upper back. They would wear these war bonnets into the battle.

Each feather in a war bonnet was a symbol, and a warrior could not wear certain feathers until he earned them. The eagle's feather, for instance, was a symbol of courage. Only by acting with bravery in battle would a warrior earn the right to wear the eagle's feather in his war bonnet.

You can make a war bonnet out of poster board.

SUPPLIES

- poster board
- scissors
- crayons or magic markers
- stapler
- tape
- string

ran away to the Great Plains; but most of them spread to the region by trade. The Native Americans living in that region soon discovered that the horses were yet another tool that could help them in many ways.

A horse-drawn travois.

Because horses were much bigger and stronger than dogs, the Native Americans of the Great Plains were able to use

1 Start by cutting the poster board into many different feathers. If you have only one color of poster board than you may want to color some of these feathers with crayons or magic markers. After you've got a bunch of different colored feathers, write a word on each of them to signify its meaning. One feather might be for bravery, for example, while others might be for intelligence or speed.

2 Next, cut a strip of poster board long enough that you can wrap it around your forehead like a headband. Staple its ends so that it fits your head, then staple or tape your feathers onto the inside of the headband.

3 Staple or tape a few pieces of string to the bottom of your head band, and attach feathers to the ends of the strings so that they dangle down the back of your neck and over your ears.

Words to Know

bullboat: a round boat made from a frame of willow branches covered in buffalo hide

species: a distinct population of similar organisms that usually interbreed only among themselves

larger *travois* for the horses to pull as they migrated with the buffalo herds. This enabled the Plains people to carry more supplies on hunts. The bigger *travois* were also used to carry infants and small children, making the journey easier for their mothers and fathers. Another great benefit of horses was that they allowed the Native Americans to cover more ground—which was useful when exploring and when hunting buffalo. On foot, people can't keep up with buffalo, but on horseback, they could not only keep up with buffalo, but steer them in whatever direction they wanted the buffalo to go. Horses became most important to the Native Americans in the Great Plains when tribes from the East started making their way inland to the Great Plains region. Much fighting ensued over territory and hunting rights, and horses became an important tool of war, especially to tribes like the Comanche.

The Comanche became the most expert horsemen in all of the Americas. They prized their horses the way someone today might value an expensive car, but they also considered their horse a loyal friend. They bred their horses to create the strongest, fastest horses possible. Owning several horses was a sign of wealth. In one unique case, a

Comanche tribe with 2,000 people is said to have owned more than 15,000 horses.

War party on horseback.

Before going into battle, a Comanche warrior would put war paint on his own face *and* on the face of his horse. The horse became the Comanche's part-ner in battle, not just a tool of transportation. Warriors would practice riding their horses for hours and hours, day after day, perfecting stunts and maneuvers that would help them in battle.

When a fellow warrior was injured on the ground, for example, a Comanche would ride quickly to him and—without even slowing down—reach down and scoop him up with one arm. This was a ma-neuver they practiced often, and it helped save many lives.

The Comanche developed a technique called the sideways maneu-ver that let them ride their horses without using their hands. To ac-complish this, a Comanche would strap a sling made of buffalo hide around his horse's neck. While riding, the warrior would lean for-ward and rest his elbow in the sling, and then he would hook one foot over the horse's back. He could keep moving with the horse this way, and both of his hands would be free to shoot arrows. Sometimes, he even surprised his enemies by shooting from between the horse's legs instead of from over its head.

To prepare for battle, Comanche warriors of-ten sang war songs and other types of songs at tribal gatherings. Music was a large part of the culture of the Great Plains tribes. They sang songs to lull their babies to sleep, to show love and affection, and even to communicate with-out words. Music was a valuable tool of communication for Native Americans all across the Americas.

Which Native American tribe was known for excellence in breeding horses?

THE LEWIS AND CLARK EXPEDITION

Meriwether Lewis

William Clark

Many of the details we know today about how the Great Plains tribes lived come from notes taken by two men: Meriwether Lewis and William Clark. From 1804 to 1806, Lewis and Clark traveled from the St. Louis, Missouri area, all the way up to North Dakota, and then west to Washington. They were sent by President Thomas Jefferson to explore these areas and take notes about the people and places they discovered. The president was interested in learning what natural resources the land offered as he considered expanding the young United States of America across the continent. In particular, he wanted to know if the Missouri River could be used as a major transportation route to move goods by boat all the way to the Pacific Ocean.

On a mission of science and discovery, Lewis and Clark posed no immediate threat to the Native American tribes they encountered. They came in peace, so the Native Americans responded kindly—in many cases helping the expedition quite a bit. Great Plains tribes helped Lewis and Clark identify different **species** of animals and plants so they could record the proper names in writing. They also told them the best routes to travel, making their journey much easier than it otherwise might have been.

The route taken by Lewis and Clark.

SACAGAWEA

One Native American was especially helpful to the Lewis and Clark expedition. Her name was Sacagawea. She was a Shoshone Indian, born in the Rocky Mountains. At about age 10, she was kidnapped by the Hidatsa, who eventually sold her to a French-Canadian trader named Toussaint Charbonneau. Charbonneau later became her husband. They were in the Dakotas when they met Lewis and Clark.

The explorers needed to trade with the Native Americans there, and they knew they would need to do more trading as they headed west through Sacagawea's homeland. It was decided that she might be helpful to their journey as an interpreter. She did not speak English, but she did speak French. Sacagawea would talk with the many Native American groups they encountered who spoke Shoshone or Hidatsa and then translate their words into French, which her husband, Charbonneau, would translate into English, so that Lewis and Clark could understand.

Statue of Sacagawea guiding Lewis and Clark.

Sacagawea proved so helpful that she accompanied the Lewis and Clark expedition all the way to the Pacific Ocean and back. Her mere presence helped the explorers significantly, for many of the tribes they encountered had never seen white men before. Had Lewis and Clark not been traveling with a Native American woman, it's very possible that the tribes they encountered would have become hostile out of fear.

Who were Lewis and Clark?

Sacagawea was a comforting presence and good interpreter. She also helped the explorers by showing them trails and shortcuts that she remembered

How did Sacagawea help the Lewis and Clark expedition?

from her childhood, and by helping them find plants for food and medicine.

When the expedition ended, Sacagawea was not paid for the work she had done. Instead, her husband was given $500.33 and 320 acres of land. Many historians believe that Sacagawea died soon after, at the young age of 25, but others argue that she lived under a different name for many decades, until the ripe old age of 100.

Had Sacagawea lived that long, she would have witnessed the aftermath of the Lewis and Clark expedition, which was not favorable to her native people. Based on Lewis and Clark's reports, many white settlers decided to move west, further into Native American lands, causing problems between settlers and the native people already living there. Settlers and sportsmen killed off many of the buffalo that the Great Plains tribes survived on.

You'll read more about the fate of the Great Plains tribes, and other tribes across the continent, in chapter 9.

THE SOUTHWEST AND MESOAMERICAN TRIBES

◆

THE HOHOKAM, MOGOLLON, ANASAZI, MAYA, AZTEC, HOPI, APACHE, AND NAVAJO

The tribes living in what is now the southwestern United States and northern Mexico adapted to the harsh desert climate, which meant great heat during the days and frigid nights through most of the year. The relative lack of water made farming a challenge, but it also made clay plentiful. This abundance of clay played a major role in how these tribes evolved. Many of these tribes learned to make pottery and even **adobe** buildings called pueblos, which eventually gave rise to the first great North American cities like **Tikal**, **Teotihuacán**, and **Tenochtitlán**.

Some experts believe that the Native Americans who lived in the southwestern United States were descendants of those from **Mesoamerica**, a region extending south and east from central Mexico to include parts of Guatemala, Belize, Honduras, and Nicaragua.

Anasazi pottery design.

Words to Know

adobe: sun-dried brick, or the clay from which these bricks are made

Tikal: a city whose name means "Place of Voices," built in present-day Guatemala around 200 BCE and spanning 23 square miles; it housed as many as 100,000 to 200,000 Maya people

Teotihuacán: a city whose name means "Abode of the Gods," populated by as many as 200,000 Aztecs and spanning about eight square miles

Tenochtitlán: an Aztec city built on Lake Texcoco that eventually housed about 200,000 people

Mesoamerica: the region that includes parts of Mexico and Central America, inhabited by various Native American civilizations

Hohokam: the "Vanished Ones" who dominated the present-day Southwest for 2,000 years, starting around 400 BCE and lasting until about 1500 CE

irrigation: the process of supplying crops with water by means of ditches or artificial channels, or by sprinklers

Gulf of Mexico

Mesoamerica

Pacific Ocean

This belief stems from the fact that tribes in the southwestern United States displayed lifestyles similar to Mesoamerican civilizations, like the Maya and Olmec.

Some of these lifestyle similarities include the cultivation of maize, writing with hieroglyphics, making books out of deerskin, using complex calendars, studying the stars, and playing ball games on stone courts. Other links between these cultures can be seen in their clay pottery, reed baskets, sandals, and cotton cloth. And still other likenesses exist in their networks of roads and irrigation systems.

THE THREE SOUTHWEST CULTURES

Within the approximate areas of New Mexico, Arizona, Colorado, and Utah, three cultures emerged. Each culture was different, but all had customs and tools similar to those discovered in nearby Mesoamerica. The earliest culture of the southwestern United States was known as the **Hohokam**, a word that means "Vanished Ones." The Hohokam dominated the region for 2,000 years, from about 400 BCE to about 1500 CE. The Hohokam people were **irrigation** farmers, growing maize and other crops for the majority of their food. They learned to control and use what water they had in the desert by building dams out of the muddy, clay earth, and by building floodgates out of woven mats they strung across waterways such as the Gila River in Arizona.

As farmers, their primary goal was to ensure the survival of their crops. The Hohokam were smart about this: Their irrigation canals were narrow and deep, like rivers, instead of wide and shallow, like puddles. This helped to prevent the water in the canals from evaporating in the hot desert sun. To keep the water from seeping into the dirt along the sides of the canals, the Hohokam lined each canal with clay that would harden, making their canals like the water pipes we use today.

East of where the Hohokam lived, along the Rocky Mountains from Colorado through New Mexico, the first major culture was the **Mogollon**. They were hunters and gatherers who lived in the mountains from about 300 BCE to 1300 CE, when other tribes began to move into their territory.

What modern-day countries does Mesoamerica include?

Mogollon pit house.

Understanding
Irrigation

In some parts of the world, such as the desert lands where the Hohokam farmers lived, there is not enough water in the land to keep important crops alive, so irrigation is essential. People who live in these places have to create irrigation systems to ensure that crops receive the water they need. Irrigation systems can vary from simple sprinklers to long, deep canals. The type of system that works best often depends on the type of ground in which the crop is planted. The grass outside your school, for instance, can probably be watered by a sprinkler, but acres and acres of crops might need irrigation ditches to provide enough water for growth.

You can experiment with different irrigation systems by planting seeds in containers of different shapes, materi-

SUPPLIES

- planting containers of different shapes, sizes, and/or material, for example: tall and narrow, wide and shallow, paper, clay, plastic
- seeds
- potting mix
- plastic wrap

Because their environment provided trees, the Mogollons used trees to make tools more than the Hohokam. Like the Hohokam, though, the Mogollons had to contend with the same desert climate— hot days and cold nights. As a result they developed shelters known as pit houses. They started these houses by digging a hole, the bottom of which served as the floor. Next, they'd frame the walls and roof with saplings before covering them with mud-based plaster. Having the floor of the living area below ground helped insulate their homes

als, and sizes, and watching how well the seeds grow. You can use any kind of seeds, from flowers to tomatoes, but you should plant the same kind of seeds in each container and water them the same amount every day.

1 Fill each container with potting mix and plant a few seeds in each container. Cover with plastic.

2 Water each container, and then watch for signs that the dirt is getting dry every one, two, or three days.

3 Keep the soil moist and your containers out of direct sunlight until your seeds germinate. Once you have seedlings you can remove the plastic and start to move them into more direct light. You can leave them in direct light more and more each day for about a week until they are used to full sunlight.

4 Throughout the process keep a notebook to record your observations every day. Which of your containers does a better job of retaining water and which of your seeds grows faster? Based on these observations you will be able to determine which type of container allows for the best irrigation.

from unpleasant weather, and during the coldest times of year, the earthen floor retained the heat from fires.

The Mogollon culture thrived until the emergence of the third original Southwest culture, the **Anasazi**, who conquered the Mogollons. The Anasazi lived in pit houses, just like those of the Mogollons, until they learned to build greater structures out of adobe, a type of natural clay that dries in the sun and becomes as hard as brick. Eventually, the Anasazi would build aboveground adobe buildings

What does Hohokam mean?

The remains of Pueblo Bonito.

called **pueblos** that were as big as modern apartment buildings and capable of housing as many as a thousand people. These pueblos had holes in their ceilings for entering and exiting. Ladders allowed people to climb in and out and from room to room across the sprawling structure.

One of the most famous of the Anasazi structures is called Pueblo Bonito, or "The Beautiful Village." Many scientists consider it the greatest architectural achievement by Native Americans on U.S. territory, though there are other ruins, including Mesa Verde, that are also considered especially significant. You can visit Pueblo Bonito's ruins today in Chaco Canyon, in the northwest part of New Mexico. You'll also see evidence there of the old pit houses, which the Anasazi later turned into chambers called **kivas** and used for ceremonies.

Who were the **Mogollons?**

THE FIRST GREAT CITIES

Around the same time that these southwestern United States civilizations were taking their first steps toward becoming small cities, about 200 CE, Native Americans farther south in modern-day Mexico and Guatemala were already living in huge cities. Many archaeologists believe that the cities of the **Maya** and **Aztec** people in the south influenced the northern tribes with a desire to build bigger, better settlements. A single glimpse into life in the Aztec and Maya cities

An Aztec city.

Words to Know

Mogollon: the hunting and gathering civilization that existed in the Rocky Mountain region from about 300 BCE until about 1300 CE

Anasazi: the group of Native Americans who conquered the Mogollons and built great structures out of adobe; their name means "ancient people" in the Hopi language

pueblo: a type of communal village consisting of one or more flat-roofed structures of stone or adobe, arranged in terraces and housing a number of families

kiva: a large room used for religious and other purposes by the Hopi

Maya: a tribe with a highly developed civilization that dominated the Yucatan, Belize, and northern Guatemala

Aztec: the people who lived in present-day Mexico and had an advanced civilization before their conquest by Cortes in 1519

aqueduct: a large pipe or conduit made for bringing water from a distant source

cistern: a large receptacle for storing water

stelae: upright stone slabs or pillars engraved with inscriptions or designs and used as monuments and grave markers

would no doubt have made a powerful impression on anyone visiting there from the north.

The first great Native American city of the Americas began its rise in Guatemala around 200 CE. It spanned 23 square miles and was called Tikal, or "Place of Voices" or "Place of Tongues" in Maya. Experts believe as many as 100,000 to 200,000 Maya lived in Tikal among its palaces, temples, ball courts, and plazas. The city's structures were connected by **aqueducts** and **cisterns** that provided fresh water to residents much the way underground pipes do for city residents today.

Tikal contained about 200 stone monuments known as *stelae*. These are upright stone slabs inscribed with words or a design. In the case of the

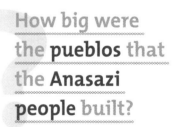

How big were the **pueblos** that the **Anasazi people** built?

A Maya stelae.

Create Your Own
Hieroglyphics

Hieroglyphics are line drawings of pictures or symbols that represent words, syllables, or sounds. The Maya carved them into slabs of rock to tell stories.

Hieroglyphics can be difficult to understand, especially if you do not know the history and beliefs of the people who created them. For instance, a picture of an eagle might make you think that someone flew somewhere, or that someone saw a soaring bird in the sky. In truth, the people who created the hieroglyphics may have believed the eagle to be a brave animal, and had therefore drawn its picture to show that a person fought well during battle. Understanding a culture is often essential to understanding the hieroglyphics that come from it.

You can tell your own stories by creating your own set of hieroglyphics. For instance, you might draw a hieroglyphic account of your morning with pictures that represent getting out of bed, eating breakfast, and brushing your teeth. What hieroglyphics might work for those scenes? Perhaps an unmade bed, a fried egg, and a toothbrush.

1 Think about what you want to write a story about, then make up a bunch of hieroglyphics that you can use tell the story. Using these hieroglyphic symbols of your own, write a story—either an account of something that happened to you today, a memorable event in your life, or of a game you have played in the past. See how many hieroglyphic symbols you can reuse from sentence to sentence within your story. Try to keep your language as simple as possible, and then show your creations to friends and see if they understand what you've "written."

SUPPLIES
- pen or pencil
- scrap paper
- construction paper

Maya monuments, the slabs were carved with elaborate **hieroglyphics** that described the lives and achievements of city rulers.

The stelae of Tikal were impressive, but not as impressive as the pyramids in the city—some of which were probably the tallest man-made structures built by Native Americans. Imagine the backbreaking work of laying massive stone upon stone to build these pyramids, all without the benefit of modern-day machinery.

Nobody knows why, but around 900 CE, the city of Tikal began to fall into ruin. Historians suggest warfare, drought, or overpopulation as possible causes. Around that same time another of the first great cities, Teotihuacán, was also in decline.

Teotihuacán, which was about 30 miles northeast of present-day Mexico City, was built around 100 CE. Eventually it spanned about eight square miles and housed as many as 200,000 residents. The Aztec people lived in Teotihuacán, which means "City of the Gods," but they did not build it—and nobody's quite sure who did. One thing is for certain, though: Teotihuacán was a powerful regional force, so powerful that some historians equate it with its contemporary city across the ocean, Imperial Rome.

Teotihuacán was constructed on an eight-square-mile grid and separated into quadrants. The two-mile-long Avenue of the Dead was the main street that ran through the city. The city's streets and alleys were

Avenue of the Dead.

Words
to Know

glyph: a picture or symbol representing a word, syllable, or sound; used instead of alphabetical letters

talud-tablero: a building technique with sloped walls covered with decorative panels

Quetzalcoatl: the Feathered Serpent, one of the main gods of all Mesoamerican civilizations

chinampas: floating gardens used by the Aztecs in the city of Tenochtitlán

paved in stone, and the temples were almost as steep as mountain cliffs. It is believed that the people of Teotihuacán read and wrote books, counted numbers using bars and dots, observed a 260-day calendar, and drank chocolate from vases.

The buildings of Teotihuacán were created with a technique called **talud-tablero**, in which the walls are sloped and covered with decorative panels. Just like in the Maya city of Tikal, the most prominent structures in Teotihuacán were the pyramids. One such pyramid, the Pyramid of the Sun, remains the third largest pyramid in the world; another, the Temple of **Quetzalcoatl**, is inside the Ciudadela complex at the southern end of the Avenue of the Dead.

As with Tikal, nobody knows why the city of Teotihuacán fell into ruin before 1,000 CE. But not long after that, around 1,325 CE, construction began on a third major city of the Americas: Tenochtitlán.

Aztec history had prophesied that its people would find the site for their great city at the spot where they encountered an eagle perched

The Temple of Quetzalcoatl.

The God Quetzalcoatl

Quetzalcoatl is to the religion of Mesoamerica what Jesus Christ is to Christianity. Both are prophesied to return to the earth.

The story of Quetzalcoatl varies from tribe to tribe across Mesoamerica. In all of the stories, however, he is the Feathered Serpent, one of the main gods of all civilization. He is the god of the morning star, and he created mankind from the bones of failed civilizations. He invented books and the calendar, and he created maize for everyone to eat.

The Maya and Aztecs worshiped the Feathered Serpent; its legacy, however, was upheld by tribes and civilizations for about 2,000 years after their decline.

on a cactus devouring a snake. As the Aztecs moved from the west into the northern part of what is now known as the Mexican Highlands, they encountered that exact scene at Lake Texcoco.

The Aztecs immediately set about building Tenochtitlán right in the middle of the lake. They did this by inventing **chinampas**, or floating gardens, which were bunches of twigs tied together with mud stacked on them. These chinampas could be anchored to the lake bottom, creating foundations for building structures, or they could be towed around the lake until the roots of the plants on them grew deep enough to anchor themselves into the lake bottom. The technique worked: Tenochtitlán eventually grew big enough to house and feed as many as 200,000 people.

Sun Stone, or Calendar Stone, of the Aztecs.

The Aztecs who lived in Tenochtitlán also built causeways that connected their man-made island to the mainland. The causeways kept the lake's freshwater supply separate from nearby salty lakes. The Aztecs also built canals that allowed them to move between the chinampas in boats.

Tenochtitlán flourished for a long time, until 1521, when Spanish explorer Hernando Cortez and his army captured the city and destroyed most of its original buildings.

MODERN DESCENDANTS

The Pima and Tohono O'Odham tribes were descendents of the Hohokam. They lived near the Gila River in Arizona, but their area of influence extended all the way down to Sonora, Mexico. The two tribes were close allies, and they were both expert makers of watertight baskets. The Tohono O'Odham are also known as the **Papago**—a name that comes from the word *papah*, meaning "beans," and *ootam*, meaning "people." The name **Pima** means "no," and was incorrectly used to describe the tribe by Christian missionaries. Unfortunately, the name stuck.

Pima basket designs.

Pima history tells of a rainstorm that caused massive flooding and killed all but one member of the tribe, a chief whose son took 20 wives and had enough children of his own to help the tribe survive. According to the traditions of the tribe, an owl carried the souls of the dead away, and so they feared hooting birds, believing they were signs of impending death.

Typical vegetation of the southwest desert, saguaro cactus and scrub.

Pimas and Death

The Pima followed a unique custom whenever a member of their tribe died. They buried their dead men and women in a sitting position, facing east, with their favorite foods and possessions for the journey to the afterworld. Everything else a person had—including their house—was destroyed upon their death. Even animals, such as horses, were sacrificed as part of this ritual.

No other members of the tribe were permitted to speak the deceased person's name until long after their death, and no future children were allowed to be named after the deceased person. The Pima believed that even uttering a deceased person's name brought back all the sorrow associated with their death.

The Pima were peaceful people. They farmed maize, beans, and cotton to maintain their existence. When attacked, however, they would fight back with stone, glass, and iron spear points on their arrows. They also used war clubs and shields made of rawhide.

The Tohono O'Odham of southern Arizona were similar to the Pima, in that they were peaceful farmers. They also foraged for desert plants, however, such as the giant cactus, to survive. They used a tool called a *kuibit*—a long pole made of dried saguaro cactus ribs—to knock the sweet fruit off of flowering saguaro cacti. They ate the fruit raw, like candy, or they boiled it to make syrup or jam. Sometimes they fermented the fruit to make wine, or dried it out and ground it into a powder that could be mixed with water, sort of like the lemonade packets that you find in supermarkets today.

Perhaps the best-known descendants of the Anasazi culture were the Hopi, a tribe whose name means "Peaceful Ones." The Hopi lived in Arizona, building their pueblos on **mesas** that could be easily defended against enemy tribes. These settlements were similar to the pueblos built by their Anasazi ancestors.

Like the Anasazi, the Hopi farmed corn, squash, beans, and tobac-

Papago basket designs.

Hopi ceremonial sash.

Words to Know

Papago: close allies of the Pima who lived in and around Arizona; they call themselves Tohono O'Odham

Pima: expert makers of watertight baskets who lived near the Gila River in Arizona

mesa: a widespread flat area at high elevation with one or more cliff-like sides

dibble: a digging stick used by Hopi farmers

co. To plant corn in the desert earth where they lived, the Hopi used a digging stick called a **dibble**. It was a long stick that allowed each farmer to create a narrow hole at least a foot deep. The depth of the hole depended on how far down the damp subsoil was. Once the dibble reached the damp subsoil, the farmer would drop 10 to 20 seeds into the hole and pack them in tightly with dirt. This created a cool, wet environment protected from the desert sun, and the seeds sprouted deep roots that served as strong anchors after the plants burst through the topsoil and had to hold their ground against the desert wind.

Once the corn was harvested, it would be used to cook *piki*, a paper-thin bread that the Hopi people dipped into stews of squash, beans, wild sagebrush, milkweed, watercress, and dandelions. To make *piki* batter, cornmeal was mixed with water, and wood ash. Then, the cook heated a slab of sandstone called a *duma* by placing it above a fire. When the *duma* was just the right temperature, the cook would spread the batter on it by hand, then quickly lift it off with her fingers before it burnt. She would then roll the piki into a cylinder shape before it had time to dry out and crack into little pieces. Good *dumas* were prized possessions, passed down for generations, and being able to make proper *piki* was a highly valued skill.

WARRIORS FROM THE NORTH

The Pima, Tohono O'Odham, Hopi, and other tribes in the Southwest United States lived in relative peace until the

Hopi design for a woman's shawl.

Navajo and Apache tribes began to migrate there from Canada some-time after 1000 CE. The warriors of the Navajo and Apache tribes raided both the pueblos and the early Spanish settlements in the area, and quickly came to dominate the region. The Navajo people lived in Arizona, New Mexico, and part of Utah, while the Apaches spread across the southern Plains into Colorado, Arizona and New Mexico, right down into northern Mexico.

The Apache were nomadic people, which means they didn't settle in one place for long periods of time. The Apache hunted deer and buffalo, and lived in shelters called wikiups. Apache wikiups were dome-shaped, and were made of wooden poles covered with brush or reed mats. A smoke hole in the top of the wikiup served as a chim-ney for the fire pit in the center of the floor. Some Apache covered their wikiups with buffalo hides. The Apache were known as fierce warriors, and throughout history fought first with neighbor-ing tribes, then with the Spanish, who tried to kidnap Apaches to work as slaves in silver mines in Mexico. The Apache had a repu-tation for amazing endurance. Some stories say Apache warriors could run fifty miles without stopping.

The Navajo called themselves simply "Dineh," or "the people." Navajos lived in houses called hogans. Each hogan was hexagonal or octagonal (six or eight-sided) and was built with the door facing east. The Navajo built their hogans from logs, and finished them with mud plaster. The first Navajo were farmers, who grew corn, beans, and other crops. Over time, the Navajo became shepherds, and raised and herded sheep in addition to farming. The Navajos often clashed with

Apache basket designs.

Create Your Own
Navajo Dry Painting

One of the great artistic endeavors of the Navajo people was the creation of sand paintings. These works of art were often so large and detailed that they took 15 men as long as a full day to make. They were created to remove spells, which they believed caused famine, disease, untimely deaths, and other bad things to occur.

The artists would start by finding an area of level ground, preferably dirt that was uniform in color. Next they would sprinkle colored sand within the bounds of a circle. Depending on the spells that needed to be removed, the artists would create different pictures on top of this circle with red, white, yellow, black, and blue powders. The powders were made from ground charcoal, sandstone, gypsum, and ocher.

When the dry painting was complete, any person who needed a spell removed would sit on it. A shaman would then dance around the person, shaking a rattle, praying, and chanting.

When the ceremony was complete, the painting—along with the offending spells—would be destroyed, but each participant would keep a pinch of sand for themselves, believing that it now contained healing powers.

You can make a dry painting by using colored sand from any arts and crafts store.

Say you want to remove a spell that you think is making a boy or girl in your class act meanly. You could use the colored sands to create a picture of him or her, and then dance around the picture with a rattle, chanting for him or her to be nicer.

SUPPLIES
- colored sand
- a large piece of posterboard

Spanish settlers from what is now New Mexico, and later with other settlers and gold prospectors.

Navajo and Apache warriors who raided existing settlements were seeking everything from cotton blankets and woven baskets to pottery, turquoise beads, farming tools, silver baubles, sheep, and horses. They were particularly aggressive in capturing sheep, which they learned to shear for wool that they spun into yarn for cloth and blankets.

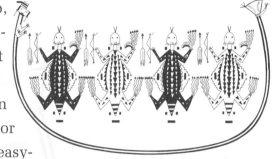

Navajo sand painting.

The most famous of the Apache warriors was a man called Geronimo. His original name was Goyathlay, or "The One Who Yawns," given to him because of his easy-going nature. Married at age 17, he lived a peaceful life until he turned 27, in 1858. That's the year Mexican troops trying to take over Apache lands murdered Goyathlay's entire family. He swore revenge.

Mexican soldiers nicknamed him Geronimo (the reason remains a mystery), which is Spanish for Jerome. The soldiers warned all their people about Geronimo, who led raids on Mexican and U.S. settlements until he finally surrendered in 1886.

After U.S. soldiers took control of Apache lands, leaders back East sought out Geronimo as a symbol of the Native American heritage that had once existed in the Southwest. President Theodore Roosevelt even brought him to Washington, D.C., in 1905 to participate in the inaugural parade. Souvenir bows, arrows, and pins were sold bearing Geronimo's likeness.
He died in 1909.

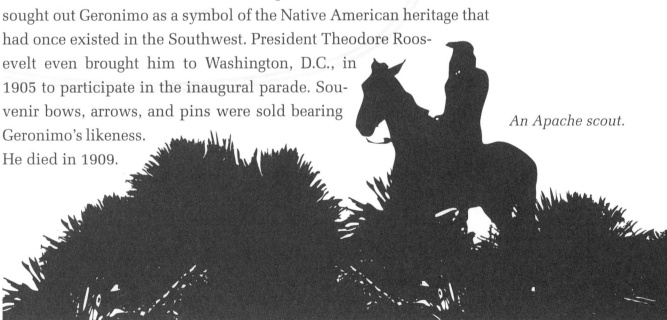

An Apache scout.

Create Your Own
Navajo Jewelry

The Navajo are well known for their art, especially sand painting, weaving, and jewelry making. In this activity you will make beads that represent the sacred colors of the Navajo compass: north is black, south is turquoise, east is white, and west is yellow.

1 Cut a piece of string approximately two feet long. Attach a piece of masking tape at the end so the beads won't fall off the end of the string.

2 Cut four triangles measuring 1 inch at the base by approximately 3 inches high out of each color of construction paper. You'll have 12 triangles.

3 Take a toothpick and roll the base of the triangle around the toothpick very tightly. Put a dot of white glue on the rolled up paper and hold it for several seconds. Take out the toothpick. You should have a tube-shaped bead.

4 Paint a clear coat of nail polish on each bead. Let dry.

5 When all the beads are dry, put them on the string. Remove the masking tape and tie the ends of the string together. Make sure the string is long enough to go over your head before you tie it!

SUPPLIES

- construction paper in the following colors: black, turquoise (or light blue), white, and yellow
- string
- toothpick
- white glue
- scissors
- clear nail polish
- masking tape

THE PACIFIC NORTHWEST TRIBES

THE NOOTKAS, MAKAHS, AND TLINGITS

The Pacific Northwest is one of the most beautiful regions of North America. Sprawling forests of deep-green fir trees blanket the mountains, whose snow-capped peaks reach beyond the clouds into the heavens. Just offshore are chains of islands and protected harbors, and all along the coast is a network of trails where hikers can photograph black bears, bald eagles, and more.

It's no surprise that the word *rugged* is often used when describing this part of the continent, as the terrain is dense with forests, mountains, and rock formations that make farming difficult or even impossible. Because of these conditions, the Native Americans that settled there had to focus on hunting, gathering, and fishing to

A grizzly bear catching salmon.

survive. Eventually, as the tribes came into contact with one another, they also used trade as a tool of survival.

There were more than two dozen tribes in the Pacific Northwest, including the Haida, Tsimshian, Tlingit, Tillamook, Chinook, Älsé, Coos, and Coquille. They had their differences, but they had one important thing in common: fishing. Every spring, the salmon **spawn** in this part of North America. Hundreds of thousands of salmon make their way back from the ocean to the rivers where they were born to lay eggs. They swim together in schools through the region's waterways. Rivers become so clogged with fish that a person cannot take a step into the water without stepping on one. Bears often sit on the riverbanks, simply scooping their paws into the water and picking up salmon to eat, like you or I might do at a cafeteria buffet.

The fact that the salmon spawn every year at the same time made fishing in this region reliable. All of the Native American tribes that lived here developed tools for catching as many fish as possible and for preserving their catch throughout the cold winters, when finding food was difficult.

FISHING TECHNIQUES

In all of the fishing tribes of the Pacific Northwest, it was up to the men to catch the fish and the women to preserve them. The simplest way for a man to catch a fish was with his bare hands, just as the black bears did with their claws. But with so many salmon to be had, the men wanted to catch more than one fish at a time, and they invented tools to do so.

A dip net.

One of the more basic fishing tools was called a **dip net**. A man would make a Y- or V-shaped frame (or find a branch of this shape), then hang a bag of netting from this frame, with the net opening attached to the frame itself. Then, much like someone today might scoop leaves out of a swimming pool, the fisherman would use his dip net to scoop fish out of the river.

A tool that helped the Native Americans catch more fish with less effort was the **weir**. A weir is a wooden trap laid across the entire width of a stream or river. It is flat, with holes the size of those in a modern-day, chain-link fence. The holes are large enough to let the river's water flow through but too small to allow any fish from passing. The flow of the river would push the fish into the weir, where fishermen waited to collect them. Some fish got through the weirs, because the weirs weren't perfect, but most of them got caught.

Native Americans of the Pacific Northwest collected the fish caught in their weirs by spearing them with a **leister**. A leister is a spear with three prongs arranged like the points of a triangle. Because

What is a dip net?

Words to Know

spawn: to produce or deposit eggs, sperm, or young

dip net: a bag of netting suspended from a Y- or V-shaped wooden frame; used for fishing

weir: a fence or obstruction built in a river or stream to divert water or catch fish

leister: a kind of fish spear, usually with three prongs

anadromous: a fish that returns from the sea to the river it was born in to breed

redd: a spawning area of trout or salmon

lattice: an openwork structure of crossed strips or bars of wood, metal, or other material, used as a screen or support

roe: fish eggs

Weirs were not only used in the Pacific Northwest. In what is today the city of Boston, Massachusetts, scientists have found evidence of a huge weir used by Native Americans. The remnants of this weir show that those who made it found or cut sticks of wood into four-to-six-foot lengths, then whittled them sharp on one end and stuck them a few feet apart into the clay bed beneath the water. Judging by the size of this contraption, scientists estimate that 65,000 sticks were used.

HOW SALMON SPAWN

Because of their spawning ritual, salmon are **anadromous**: they return from the sea to the rivers where they were born in order to breed. Salmon swim for years and for thousands of miles throughout the ocean, but they always find their way back to the very same river where they were born. Some experts believe they navigate by way of smell; others believe they are especially sensitive to the earth's magnetic field and their brains work like a compass. Nobody knows for sure.

As salmon swim from salt water back into fresh water their appearance changes. The males develop a curved mouth with large canine teeth, and the females and males both change color, from silver to black. Some males develop a hump on their back.

The males and females form pairs as they make their way upriver. The male's job is to protect the female while the female creates a nest in the gravel riverbed by sweeping her tail back and forth across it. This spawning area, which can be as big as ten feet long by six feet wide, is called a **redd**.

Once the redd is complete, the female releases her eggs at the same time the male releases his milt, or sperm. The eggs are fertilized in the water as they float down into the redd. The female then sweeps the area with her tail again to cover and protect the fertilized eggs with gravel.

The parent salmon die soon thereafter. The eggs hatch within one to three months, and the cycle of life begins anew.

there were three sharp tips, rather than only one, it was much easier for the fisherman to spear a wriggling fish on the first try. To make it easier to see and spear fish caught in a weir in murky water, fishermen would lay slabs of white quartz on the river bottom to create a brighter backdrop.

During the bountiful weeks of spawning season, the Native Americans developed another tool for collecting salmon caught in their weirs. Latticework traps were made of wood, just like the weirs, but they were shaped like boxes or cylinders. The sides of the boxes and cylinders were crisscrossed strips of wood that formed a **lattice** pattern. The fishermen would place these latticework traps at right angles to the weirs, then stand between two traps and use their hands or a net to scoop salmon by the dozen from the edge of the weir into the traps.

The fish that escaped the weirs continued upstream to lay their eggs. Those eggs, called **roe**, made for a tasty treat (just as caviar does today) and Native Americans invented a way to collect them. Before the spawning began, fishermen would place branches from hemlock trees in the water where salmon and other fish, including herring, were known to lay their eggs. The fishermen would weigh the branches down with rocks so that they would not float away. After the fish laid their eggs, the fishermen would simply lift the branches and scoop off the roe.

How do you use a leister?

A leister.

PRESERVING THE CATCH

Native Americans of the Pacific Northwest knew that the catch they brought home would have to last throughout the winter. The women were experts at saving every last morsel.

What is a latticework trap?

For starters, they would boil the fish they wanted to eat immediately. To boil the great quantity of fresh fish caught in spawning season, women would line up canoes that had been dug out of tree trunks and fill them with water and fish. Then, us-

LONGHOUSES

One common form of housing for many tribes of the Pacific Northwest was the long-house. Longhouses were very large, communal houses where members of extended families lived together. Each clan had its own longhouse, which were sometimes as long as 100 feet or more, built from cedar planks. The long houses had an entrance door on one end of the building, and a chimney hole for smoke. Often, clans would decorate the outside of their longhouses with beautiful clan symbols. Individual fam-

ilies within a clan lived in the longhouses, separated by mats made from cedar bark to make a private space for themselves within the longhouse. Many longhouses had a community fire pit in the center of the long house, which served as a communal area. In some Pacific Northwest tribes, if the tribe built the long house, the chief or head of the tribe assigned space in the long house to individual families. In others, individual members of the tribe built long houses and assigned their family members to space within the long house.

How do you build a weir?

ing long wooden tongs, they would move rocks that had been sitting in fire into the canoes filled with water and fish until the water boiled.

As the fish boiled, their oil would rise to the top of the water. The women would skim the oil off the top of the water with wooden ladles. The oil was stored in watertight wooden boxes to be used year-round in cooking and seasoning food, making medicines, or even trading to other tribes that needed it.

Women made lamps out of the most oily fish of a catch. First they would dry the fish in the sun (the organs would dry up but the oil would remain); then they inserted a piece of string through the fish to serve as a wick. The oil in the fish would burn for a long time, creating light and even heat.

Fish drying on a rack.

Fish that were to be preserved for food throughout the year were hung outside on wooden drying frames. Before hanging the fish, the women would use a bone blade to remove the head, tail, fins, and entrails, which are the guts or insides of the fish. After each fish was prepared, it would be hung alongside thousands of others. After the fish dried in the sun, the women smoked it so that its meat would not spoil.

OTHER FOOD SOURCES

The Native Americans of the Pacific Northwest did not eat only salmon. Two tribes in particular, the Nootkas and the Makahs, were known as great whale hunters.

The Nootkas and Makahs lived on Vancouver Island and throughout the Olympic Peninsula. They built long, strong wooden canoes

Whaling crew.

for their whale hunters. Because whale meat and blubber were so important to these tribes, the whale hunters were highly regarded. The position of chief harpooner was extremely important and could only be inherited from one's father.

During the hunt, each chief harpooner carried an 18-foot-long wooden harpoon. On the harpoon's tip was a blade of mussel shells and bone spurs that jutted out like barbed hooks. Attached to the other end of the harpoon were lengths of rope connected to large floats, like balloons or buoys, made of sealskin.

The hunters would paddle their canoes out to a whale—no small feat—and position themselves so that the chief harpooner had a clear shot. Several canoes would attack the same whale at once to increase their odds of a successful hunt. When the chief harpooners were in position, they would try to spear. If it was a lucky day, more than one of the harpoons would stick into the great mammal.

The wounded whale would dive beneath the surface, taking the embedded harpoons with it. The hunters would throw overboard the sealskin floats that were connected to each harpoon. The floats had two purposes: they made it harder for the whale to swim below the surface, and they prevented it from sinking after it died. Once the giant animal stopped breathing, the hunters would paddle back to shore, towing their catch behind them.

It was a joyous occasion when the Nootka and Makah hunters returned to the beach with a whale in tow. Every member of the tribe would take part in the butchering process, and every part of the whale would be saved for use. The meat and skin were eaten, the sinews, or tendons, were braided and turned into rope, the intestines were used as containers to preserve food, and the blubber was used to make oil for candles.

How do you hunt a whale?

TRIBAL INTERACTION

The fact that so much of the food harvesting occurred during one season in the Pacific Northwest gave the Native Americans who lived there time to focus on saving up wealth to obtain status, and preserving tribal history for future generations.

One way to acquire wealth was through trading with other tribes. Trade was an enormous part of society for many tribes. The Tlingits not only traded their own goods, but also acted as middlemen for surrounding tribes, taking a share of the profit for their efforts. Some of the trading trips made by Tlingits took them days on end, and they often had to cross dangerous rivers and tall mountains—in terrible weather and with packs on their backs that weighed up to 100 pounds. Some Tlingits made these trad-

What is a **sealskin float?**

Create Your Own
X-ray Art

In Oregon, the Washo and Wishram tribes passed the time between fishing and hunting by drawing, painting, and carving. The artists among these tribes would not just draw or carve the outline of, say, a fish. They would fill that outline with everything they believed to be inside the fish—the bones, organs, and spirits—so that their finished artwork looked like something you might see in a modern X-ray machine.

Choose an animal that was plentiful in the Pacific Northwest during the time the Washo and Wishram tribes lived there—salmon, black bear, and the bald eagle are a few—and draw it as the Washo or Wishram artists might have. Be sure to research your chosen animal's anatomy so that you can be sure to represent its insides properly.

SUPPLIES
- paper
- markers or crayons

ing trips during winter, when they had to wear snowshoes and keep a sharp lookout for wild animals. They certainly earned their profit!

Some of the trade between Pacific Northwest tribes occurred via waterways, with Native Americans from many tribes loading their goods into their dugout canoes that went up and down the coast. Just as the Tlingit acted as middlemen for trade that required travel over land, the Chinook tribe controlled the flow of trade on rivers. It is even believed that they exacted tolls from tribes that canoed past their settlements.

The large profits that were made through trade in the Pacific Northwest eventually led members of these tribes to set their sights on acquiring wealth. Many people in this region wanted to possess more than their neighbors, because this would gain them a higher social rank.

Those who succeeded in becoming rich, flaunted what they had by holding a **potlatch**, a dinner. During these occasions the host family gave away as many possessions as possible—not out of kindness but to show how much they had. It was believed that the more a person gave away, the more highly he or she should be thought of in society. The richest people in the Tlingit tribes were even given a special name: Ankawoo.

Potlatches were grand ceremonies

Words to Know

potlatch: a ceremony, sometimes lasting for several days, at which a host lavishes gifts upon his guests

totem: an emblem of a family or clan, often a reminder of its ancestry; usually a carved or painted representation of such an object

totem pole: a pole or post carved and painted with totems; often erected in front of Native American dwellings

that lasted several days. Hundreds of guests would attend, some traveling several days to get there. The hosts would have prepared for several years in advance, gathering gifts to present to each guest. According to legend, at one potlatch, a host gave away about 10,000 blankets. Imagine the effort behind accumulating so many blankets, when every single one had to be handmade and transported by boat or by foot.

What is a potlatch?

TOTEM POLES

It was important to the Tlingit and other tribes of the Pacific Northwest that their family and tribal histories be passed down throughout the generations. Instead of using written words to tell their stories, they used pictures. Like the hieroglyphics found throughout Mesoamerica, which were carved in stone, the **totem poles** were pictures and symbols carved out of cedar trees.

Totem poles were often erected outside the entrance to a family's dwelling, so that everyone would know their history. When a family held a potlatch, for instance, its totem pole would help the guests understand how the family had come to acquire its wealth. The figures on the pole ranged from human faces to animals, each of which represented something different. While eagles and ravens often represented different clans, or families, crows signified intelligence.

Create Your Own
Family Totem Pole

Totem poles are meant to convey a family's history. You probably can't carve an entire tree as tall as the flagpole outside your school to create a totem pole that tells your family story, but you can use the idea of a totem pole to tell your family history.

Raven with moon

1 Ask your parents about your family tree. You want to know the names and stories of as many people as possible, including your parents, grandparents, great-grandparents, and anyone else you can learn about.

Raven stealing Beaver's lake

2 On construction paper, draw or cut out faces or animals representing each person's accomplishments. If you had a particularly brave relative, you might draw a picture of an eagle, if you had a very funny relative, you might incorporate the face of a clown, and so on. After you have created an image for each person in your family history, staple or tape the images together, one above the other, as if on a ladder.

Grandfather of Raven

Raven

3 Tape your totem pole to the wall so that it climbs as high as possible. If you want to be like the Tlingits of the Pacific Northwest, you can tape it to the wall outside the doorway to your room, so that everyone who walks by or enters will be able to look at your family history.

Beaver

Raven

SUPPLIES
- a package of construction paper
- markers or crayons
- scissors
- tape

CHAPTER 8

THE ARCTIC TRIBES

THE INUIT

Try to remember the coldest weather you have ever felt. Perhaps it was so cold that the tip of your nose hurt, and your toes turned white and went numb. Think of how thankful you were to get back inside a warm building or house that had strong windows, a solid roof, and thick siding.

Imagine living in a part of North America where the temperature falls to minus-70 degrees Fahrenheit, the ocean itself sometimes freezes six or seven feet deep, and the winds are so frigid that they can give human skin frostbite on contact. There are no trees, no plants, and no possibility of farming for sustenance. There is only solid ice and snow.

This place, known as the **Arctic**, is at the far northern edge of North America, and it is believed that

Arctic landscape.

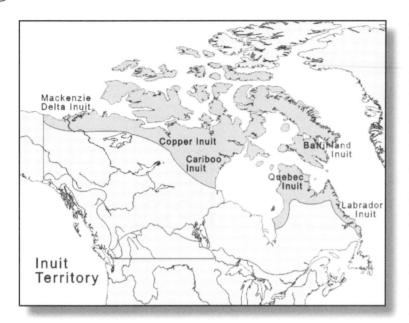

Mackenzie Delta Inuit

Copper Inuit

Cariboo Inuit

Baffinland Inuit

Quebec Inuit

Labrador Inuit

Inuit Territory

people have been living there since the earliest Native Americans arrived around 3000 BCE. They were likely the last people to cross from Asia into the Americas, and it's possible that they were trapped on ice floes that moved across the Pacific Ocean. These people did not have a house or building to warm up in like you did in your coldest memory, but they did find creative ways to adapt and survive—just like every other Native American group across the continent.

You may know the Native Americans of the north as **Eskimos**, but that is a name given to them by Algonquians farther south, a slur that means "eaters of raw meat," and a name that some people of the far north find offensive.

One Arctic tribe, known as the **Inuit**, or "the people," managed to create a sustainable culture in the frigid climate that was, at times, downright heroic. It's impossible to know why the Inuit and other Arctic tribes stayed in a land of such hardship. Some experts believe that hostile tribes to the south prevented them from migrating to a warmer climate; others feel that they simply decided to make do and never got around to moving.

What does the word *Inuit* mean?

BUILDING SHELTERS

When you imagine Inuit life, you probably think of **igloos**. These dome-shaped houses made of packed snow and ice were indeed important to the Inuit way of life, but the permanent shelters in which most Inuits lived were actually sod dwellings. With

Site of an ancient Inuit settlement.

driftwood or whalebones as frames, their walls were built of layers of sod that was collected during spring, summer, and autumn—before the deep-winter freeze. Each sod dwelling was partially underground, giving it a natural form of insulation, and all the dwellings were grouped together around a ceremonial house, or **kashim**, used only by the men of the tribe for performing rituals and ceremonies.

Igloos were built as temporary homes during seal-hunting season, a time when the Inuit tried to collect as much food as possible. Fifty to sixty people, about fifteen of whom were hunters, would leave the sod dwellings for the Arctic Ocean, where the seals lived. The elderly and the sick, and anyone who wasn't physically capable of making the long, difficult journey, would stay behind. There were no trees in seal

Words to Know

Arctic: the region around the North Pole, including the Arctic Ocean and the surrounding land north of 70 degrees latitude

Eskimo: a derogatory nickname meaning "eaters of raw meat," given to the northernmost Native Americans by the Algonquian tribes from the south

Inuit: the name the northernmost Native Americans who lived in the Arctic chose for themselves, meaning "The People"

igloo: a house or hut, usually dome-shaped, built of blocks of packed snow

kashim: a ceremony house used only by Inuit men, built in the center of a group of sod dwellings

Make Your Own
Quinzy

You can create shelter in a very cold, snowy environment, with a snow cave, or quinzy. The snow acts as an insulating shelter that helps trap your body heat. In fact, the inside of a quinzy can be warmer than 32 degrees Fahrenheit even when it is -40 degrees outside.

1 Mark out an area in the snow that is about 6 to 8 feet in diameter. The area should be relatively flat with no trees or rocks in the way.

2 If you have packs, extra brush, and a tarp, your quinzy will be much easier to build. Pile the packs and brush in the center of the quinzy area, as big as you want the interior of the quinzy to be. Cover the packs and brush with the tarp.

3 Shovel snow on top of the tarp and gear until it is covered by a foot or more of snow. DO NOT pack the snow—the snow crystals retain warmth, similar to the way a fluffy sleeping bag with more loft retains warmth better.

4 Once you have covered the mound with about a foot of snow on all sides, leave it alone for at least two hours to settle. During this time the snow will harden. Once the snow has settled and hardened, you can hollow out your living space. Dig an entrance horizontal to the ground on the side of the quinzy opposite of where the wind is blowing. It will be easier to keep the quinzy warm.

SUPPLIES

- pile of snow
- shovel
- tarp
- lots of brush and/or backpacks (optional)
- candle and matches (optional)

5 As you take snow out of the quinzy at the entrance, pile it on the outside to thicken the walls. You can also make a windbreak slightly in front of the entrance.

6 Since you built your quinzy over a mound of gear, the interior is already hollowed out. Finish digging in and take out the backpacks and brush. The tarp can fall to the floor. Smooth the interior walls. Try to taper the walls so that the walls are about 1 ½ feet thick, and the ceiling of the quinzy is about 1 foot thick. You can use a stick or a ski pole to check the thickness. Remember: the thicker the walls, the warmer the quinzy. Once you have hollowed out your living space, smooth the interior to make it as dome shaped on the inside as possible.

7 Place the candle on the middle of the floor of the quinzy and light it. Leave the candle burning for 15 to 20 minutes. This will cause the walls of the quinzy to melt very slightly, then freeze, glazing them over.

8 Make a few ventilation holes in the ceiling of your quinzy with a stick or pole. Glaze the holes with the candle, similar to the way you glazed the walls. Check the ventilation holes often.

9 Once the walls are glazed leave the quinzy alone for an hour or so. This will allow the entire structure to harden. While you're waiting, you can cut some pine boughs to use as flooring. You'll want several inches of boughs or other insulating material between you and the floor so you'll stay warm.

10 When you go inside your quinzy, block the entrance with boughs, your backs, or even snow. Remember to brush off any snow from your clothes, since the snow will melt in the warmth of your shelter and make you wet. You can light a candle in the quinzy for added warmth, but you'll probably be surprised at how warm you'll be!

Reminder: bring a shovel with you in your quinzy, since you may have to dig yourself out.

An Inuit man outside his igloo. Note the leister behind his shoulder.

country from which to build houses, so the Inuits who made the trip used the only materials available: ice and snow.

To make an igloo, the builders would first clear freshly fallen, loose snow from a patch about 50 feet wide with shovels made of sealskin-covered caribou antlers. This patch would serve as the "yard" upon which the igloo would be built, with space outside for walking and doing chores. After the patch was cleared, they would draw a circle, an outline of the igloo's floor.

Next, someone would stand inside the circle and begin carving into the hard-packed snow with a knife. The goal was to loosen rectangular blocks of hard-packed snow, each about two feet long, two feet wide, and six inches thick. They would place the blocks around the circle, creating a ledge, inching the blocks closer to the center of the circle with each layer, so that they would eventually meet overhead.

While the walls were being laid inside the igloo, other workers would be outside the circle, packing loose snow into the cracks and holes left between the snow bricks. The soft snow would act like mortar between bricks, filling in the gaps and holding the bricks in place.

The next task was the digging of an entranceway, which always faced south to prevent the fierce north wind from blowing inside.

A small hole would be left in the roof for ventilation and to let candle and fire smoke escape. Sometimes, they would also leave space in the side of the igloo for a window made of a clear, freshwater ice block, which they carried with them from their sod dwellings.

Playing **Nugluktaq**

Whether the Inuits were at their temporary hunting quarters or at home in their sod dwellings, they found the time to relax and play games after a hard day's work.

A favorite game was called Nugluktaq and is one that you can easily replicate today.

1 Have an adult hold a spool of thread, high in the air. Have this adult drop the spool, but hold on to the end of the thread. The spool will spin as the thread unravels.

2 You and the other players should be waiting beneath the spool, holding long toothpicks or skewers in your hands. The goal of Nugluktaq is to be the first person to stick his or her toothpick or skewer into the hole in the spinning spool. Be careful not to poke the adult holding the string!

3 The score can be kept in single points or in batches, such as best of three attempts, best of five attempts, and so on.

SUPPLIES

- a spool of thread
- toothpicks or skewers

It only took about an hour to build an igloo. Once it was erected, the women would set about arranging the inside.

The inside of an igloo usually had a main area devoted to a sleeping platform, which was a wide mound of packed snow that stood two or three feet above the floor. Atop the snow, the women placed caribou ribs or sealskin (which is waterproof) as a protective dry layer—otherwise, the body heat of the sleeping family would have melted the snow. Then,

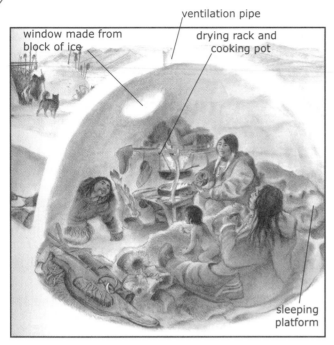

window made from block of ice

ventilation pipe

drying rack and cooking pot

sleeping platform

atop the ribs or sealskin, the women would lay caribou skins. The bottom layer of skins would be laid with the caribou hair facing downward, and the top layer of skins would be laid with the hair facing upward, for extra cushioning. Finer skins were used as mats for sitting and as place-mats for the multi-purpose dining table made of snow blocks.

Inuit people would light and heat the inside of each igloo with candles made of frozen whale blubber.

The wicks of these candles would give off a smooth, virtually smokeless flame. The heat the candle provided was not enough to melt the igloo entirely, but it would warm the inside enough that the walls of snow would drip. These drips would immediately freeze, helping to firm up the structure even more. The women would also use caribou antlers to suspend a soapstone pot above the flame. They would put frozen chunks of meat into the pot to thaw.

How do you build an **igloo**?

Once the igloo was warming up and food was being prepared, the women would set up the clothes-drying racks they had brought with them. Each drying rack was made of caribou antler and skin, and it could be used to dry clothing that became wet with snow and ice. To store and dry their ladles and sealskin containers, women would insert sticks into the igloo's walls, much like how people hang knives and other kitchen tools on their walls today.

Native Americans living in the Arctic wore goggles made from strips of wood with slits cut into them, to protect their eyes from the harsh snow and winds.

THE SEAL HUNT

As the women continued to set up camp inside the newly built igloos, the men would head out to hunt seals. A seal can swim beneath the Arctic ice for 15 to 20 minutes before it needs to come up to an air hole in the ice. It was at these air holes that the Inuit would hunt.

How does a soapstone lamp work?

Only the men hunted, though boys were often allowed to join the seal-hunting parties when they were just 10 years old.

Sled Dogs

Eskimo dogs, sometimes called "Inuit Huskies," were a hardy breed. They had muscular legs, thick necks and wide chests. Their fur—which could be any combination of white, black, reddish-brown, and gray—was "double thick" compared with other dogs' coats, even on their paws, thus helping them to stay warm in the frigid climate where they lived and worked.

The biggest males weighed as much as eighty-five pounds and could pull twice their weight while moving as far as seventy miles every day through the snow and ice. The dogs were also smart and easy to train, which made them good companions for hunters. The dogs could sniff out seal holes and even growl at polar bears to keep them still while their masters moved in closer with hunting weapons.

Today's descendants of the Eskimo dogs are called Canadian Eskimo Dogs, and they are a rare breed, with only a few hundred believed to still exist. Modern-day Canadians are so proud of the smart, obedient dogs that they put their picture on a stamp and a fifty-cent coin. In some places the dogs still pull sleds.

An Inuit hunter hunting a seal.

Each member of the hunting party used his dogs to sniff out the seals' breathing holes. When a dog found an area of fresh snow that had a breathing hole beneath it, the hunters would thrust their harpoons into the snow. Whoever's harpoon came closest to the hole was granted the right to hunt it.

First, the hunter would use an ice pick made of bear bone to widen the air hole. Next, he would stick a long, thin caribou antler down into the hole, reaching all around the bottom of the ice hole to figure out its contours. A shallower contour likely meant a seal would approach from that side, as opposed to a side that had a thick wall of ice.

Once the hunter felt he knew the angle from which the seal would approach, he covered the hole with a light layer of fresh snow, and placed a piece of frozen caribou sinew with a white feather attached to it on top. Some hunters would scratch the ice near the seal's hole with a wooden seal paw to trick any seal that might be swimming underneath the ice into thinking that one of their seal-friends was on the ice; other hunters simply waited. Sometimes the hunters had to wait for hours in the subzero Arctic temperatures before they saw that white feather move, which indicated that a seal was trying to get its nose up and into the air hole.

Why is finding a seal's air hole so important to Inuit hunters?

When the seal finally came up through the hole to breathe, the hunter lunged toward the air hole with his harpoon. Usually, it took just one try for these hunters to kill a seal that weighed anywhere from 200 to 600 pounds. This amount of meat could feed a hunter's family for weeks, and could be frozen to take with them to the next seal-hunting spot.

NEW IMMIGRANTS, MANIFEST DESTINY, AND THE TRAIL OF TEARS

I t is difficult and sad to learn the fate of the Native Americans who worked so hard to create lively and unique cultures across the Americas. Many tribes spent thousands of years developing societies and ways of life to ensure the survival of their traditions. They invented tools for hunting, building shelters, holding ceremonies, and much more. They created languages and used pictures, symbols, and carvings to tell their stories. They valued the animals with which they shared the land, and they valued the land itself.

The majority of Europeans who came to the Americas were well-intentioned people who wanted to make their own lives, and the lives of their loved ones, better. The fact is, however, their arrival in North America was the beginning of the end for the Native American way of life. As white settlers spread westward Native Americans throughout the continental U.S. were displaced from their land and nature-based culture.

PILGRIMS AND ANIMAL PELTS

Christopher Columbus, who sailed with the ships *Nína*, *Pinta*, and *Santa Maria* in 1492, is the best-known European explorer to land in North America. Columbus coined the term *Indian* because he thought he had landed in the East Indies in Asia. The islands where he actually landed were later called the West Indies. Columbus was one of many European explorers who traveled the world's oceans from the late 1400s to the early 1800s, looking for new trade routes, new places to create settlements, or new territories to control.

Columbus' fleet.

The most famous ship to reach American shores was the *Mayflower*. It landed in Plymouth, Massachusetts, in 1620, carrying pilgrims seeking a new home where they could freely practice their religion. The Pilgrims encountered some of that region's Native Americans, called the **Wampanoag**, which means "eastern people." Their meeting was peaceful. Tradition tells us that these Native Americans enjoyed the first **Thanksgiving** with the pilgrims in October 1621, following the Pilgrims' first harvest in their new homeland.

But the peaceful coexistence between the pilgrims and the Native Americans did not last. About a decade after the first Thanksgiving, as more colonists arrived and spread farther into the continent, the Native Americans grew distrustful of the white settlers. By 1675, relations had deteriorated to the point of all-out war, and the white settlers, using powerful guns, defeated the eastern tribes. The fighting between white settlers and Native Americans foreshadowed what was to come all across the continent.

What was perhaps the most successful act of defiance by

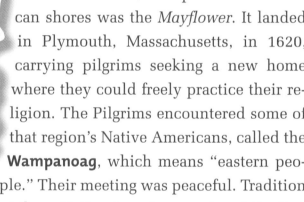

Who were and are the Wampanoag?

Reenacting the First Thanksgiving

Ironically, the feast that the pilgrims and Native Americans shared in 1621 was not actually a day of thanksgiving. The pilgrims were extremely religious, and their days of thanksgiving were spent praying and fasting. Instead, the feast was a celebration of a successful harvest and week of hunting. It lasted three days and included not just turkey, but also venison, geese, ducks, and swans. Although it was not repeated the following year, it continues to serve as the historical basis for the holiday we celebrate every year on the fourth Thursday of November.

To properly reenact the feast that the pilgrims and Native Americans shared, you must use only the foods that were available in 1621. Ask your parents if you can make a meal that would be similar to one the Pilgrims and Wampanoag would have eaten. Choose among the following ingredients: cod, bass, herring, shad, bluefish, eel, clams, lobster, mussels, wild turkey, goose, duck, crane, swan, partridge, venison, Indian corn, wheat flour, corn meal, raspberries, strawberries, grapes, plums, cherries, blueberries, gooseberries, squash, beans, walnuts, chestnuts, acorns, hickory nuts, onions, leeks, watercress, flax, sorrel, and maple syrup.

The first Thanksgiving.

the Native Americans occurred in 1680 in the Southwest. Popé, a religious leader from San Juan Pueblo in present-day New Mexico, organized and led this uprising after white settlers whipped him fiercely for refusing to convert to Christianity, and after the Spanish settlers failed to keep the Pueblo safe during a time of severe drought and disease. Under Popé's leadership, the Native Americans killed about 400 Spanish settlers, set their churches on fire, and forced them to retreat south to what is now El Paso, Texas. This uprising became known as the Pueblo Revolt.

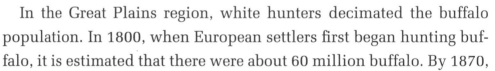

A NEW NATION

One hundred years later, on the East Coast of North America, the United States was being born. On July 4, 1776, the 13 British colonies declared their independence from England and began the process of creating their own nation. The colonists would eventually win their freedom, and floods of immigrants would come across the ocean to join them. This influx of Europeans would continue to push westward, creating new settlements on Native American lands.

All across the continent, Native Americans saw their way of life being destroyed. At first, some of them tried to engage in trade with the settlers, adopting their hunting practices of killing large numbers of animals for economic gain rather than just for survival. They would trade animal hides to the white settlers for canned food, alcohol, guns, and trinkets, and they quickly came to desire more and more of these items.

The herds of wild animals diminished as Europeans and Native Americans killed more and more animals for fur. This led to fighting among the Native American tribes themselves, as they struggled to find enough animals to maintain the high-demand fur trading business that had been thrust upon them.

Settlers home-stead in North Dakota.

In the Great Plains region, white hunters decimated the buffalo population. In 1800, when European settlers first began hunting buffalo, it is estimated that there were about 60 million buffalo. By 1870, there were about 13 million buffalo left, and by 1900, there were fewer than a thousand. This decline in buffalo was devastating to the Native Americans of the Great Plains region because they relied on the buffalo not only for food, but for tools, shelter, and clothing.

As all this happened, more and more white settlers poured into the Native

American regions across the continent, claiming land and building homes and settlements in the name of the United States of America. Eventually, the Native Americans realized their way of life was going to become extinct if they continued fighting among themselves over hunting territory and animal shortages.

Several Native American leaders rose up and began talking about rebellion against the white settlers. The settlers responded to the talk of rebellion by calling the Native Americans savages who needed to be tamed, or even eradicated from their new nation for good.

Words to Know

Wampanoag: Native Americans encountered by the *Mayflower* Pilgrims; from the Algonquian words *wampa*, meaning "dawn," and *noag*, meaning "people"

Thanksgiving: a name given to the feast that the Native Americans and pilgrims shared near Plymouth Rock, Massachusetts, after the harvest of 1621

reservation: public land set aside for a special use, such as the relocation of Native Americans in the 1800s

Trail of Tears: path of a thousand miles walked by Cherokees in 1838 when they were forced from their homelands and sent to live on reservations in present-day Oklahoma

treaty: a formal agreement between two parties relating to peace, alliance, trade, and/or property

REBELLION, GOLD, AND THE TRAIL OF TEARS

By 1829, when Andrew Jackson became president of the United States, the "Indian Problem" had become a national obsession. American settlers wanted the Native Americans' land for themselves, and the Native Americans wanted to hold onto what land they still had.

President Jackson decided that it was time to act. He signed the 1830 Indian Removal Act that had already been passed by the U.S. Congress. It stated that all Native Americans living east of the Mississippi River had to move west, to **reservations** in what is now Oklahoma. For years

JACKSON

The Cherokee people were forced to walk over 1,000 miles to live on reservations.

the Native American tribes—including the Choctaw, Chickasaw, Seminole, Creek, and Cherokee—tried to argue in the courts that they were a sovereign people who could not be forced to leave their homeland. In the end they lost their fight.

Citizens of the United States seized the Native Americans' homes and land, and in 1838 forced Cherokee men, women, and children to walk 1,000 miles from Florida and Georgia all the way to Oklahoma. The journey began in October and lasted all winter, until March. Many people died along the way. Fifteen thousand Cherokee began the forced march; 4,000 died before it ended. The Cherokee called this path the Trail of Tears.

A similar scene unfolded in the western territories of the United States starting in 1848, when prospectors discovered gold in California. The promise of riches led thousands of white settlers to the Southwest. The Native Americans who lived there fought to protect their homeland, but when the U.S. Army was sent in to destroy the fields and animals upon which the Native Americans relied for their survival, they had no choice but to surrender. In 1864, about 10,000 Navajo survivors were forced to walk nearly 200 miles to Fort Sumner, in eastern New Mexico. Many Navajo men, women, and children died.

What was the **Indian Removal Act?**

The only tribe that was somewhat successful in refusing to leave their homeland for reservations was the Seminole. Many of these people retreated to the swamps of Florida where they waged guerilla-style warfare against U.S. troops between 1835 and 1842. The Seminoles killed more than 1,500 American soldiers before the government got tired of fighting over what they considered worthless swampland.

Finding
Names from History

Although many of the Native American tribes that existed from the 1500s to the 1800s are now gone, many current place-names all across the U.S. remind us of their former presence.

Following are some tribes whose names are still used, in whole or in part, to describe locations. Look at the map and see how many places you can find that bear resemblance to the following tribal names:

Aleut	Kansa	Osage	Penobscot
Spokan	Wichita	Susquehannock	Massachuset
Mohave	Missouri	Erie	Narragansett
Dakota	Illinois	Delaware	Montauk
			Tuscarora

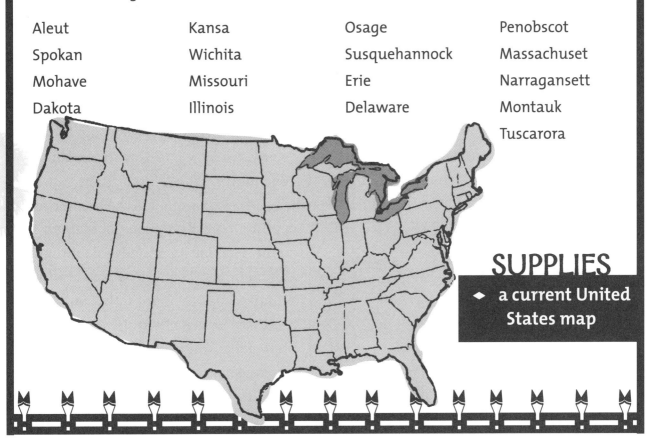

SUPPLIES
◆ a current United States map

Some Seminoles ended up on reservations in the West, but many managed to stay in their homes, where their descendants still live today.

TREATIES AND THE BATTLE OF LITTLE BIGHORN

By the 1790s, U.S. leaders had learned that getting Native Americans to hand over their homelands peacefully was much easier than taking the land by force. They began to use the legal tool of **treaties**, which they had started using in the 1780s, to take over entire territories.

From 1843 to 1852, for instance, Governor Isaac Stevenson of the Washington Territory in the Pacific Northwest negotiated 52 treaties with Native American tribes that gave the United States the legal right to 157 million acres of land in Idaho, Oregon, and

How long was the walk along the **Trail of Tears?**

Washington. Other U.S. leaders were doing the same thing all across the continent, and eventually, the United States came to control virtually every acre of Native American land.

Why did the Native Americans give up everything they had worked so hard to create? Bribery, trickery and threats combined to force them to give in to the demands of the United States. In some cases, it was because the tribes had owed money to the settlers by accepting more European goods than they could pay for in money, wampum, or animal hides. The Native Americans had promised to pay more later, and signing the treaties was a way for them to have their debts forgiven. In other cases, the Native Americans signed the treaties and gave up their land because they were promised peace and hunting rights on

Custer's Last Stand at the Battle of Little Big Horn.

the property (rights that often weren't honored). In other cases, it was simply because the Native Americans did not fully understand the English-language treaties they were signing.

The last great battle waged by Native Americans to preserve their way of life took place in 1876. The Sioux and Cheyenne had been promised the Black Hills of the Dakota Territory when they signed the Fort Laramie Treaty with the United States in 1868. It was a sacred place where they had lived and hunted for many years. But when U.S. Lieutenant Colonel George Armstrong Custer was traveling through the area, he sent word back east that there was "gold around the roots of the grass." Prospectors hoping to get rich poured into the area, setting up camps and destroying Native American lands.

Sioux leader Sitting Bull.

U.S. leaders tried to purchase the land, but the Native Americans refused to sell. The government then decided to break the Fort Laramie Treaty and declared that any Native Americans refusing to move to reservations would be considered hostile.

In March 1876, federal troops moved into the region to take over the lands. Led by two Lakota chiefs, Sitting Bull and Crazy Horse, nearly 3,000 Native Americans gathered to fight against them. They managed to kill about 225 of Custer's 600 soldiers in the Seventh Cavalry, driving the U.S. troops back. Word of the Battle of the Little Bighorn, also known as Custer's Last Stand, spread quickly, and cavalrymen from all over the United States poured into the area to help defeat the remaining Native Americans.

What led to the Battle of Little Bighorn?

Crazy Horse and Sitting Bull continued to fight, but eventually were forced to surrender and move onto reservations. They were among the last great Native American chiefs to surrender to white settlers, and Crazy Horse was killed the following year.

LEARNING MORE

The past century has certainly seen many changes for Native American tribes of all kinds, in all regions. Even those that grew to power and influence in their heyday were conquered, from the Woodlands all the way across the Great Plains to the Pacific Northwest, and everywhere in between. Today, the descendants of these tribes continue to work to keep their heritage alive through museums, archaeological digs, cultural centers, and more. Some still live on reservations, while others live in neighborhoods much like yours. They continue to hold discussions, sometimes filing lawsuits, about property rights with the government of the United States of America. In some states, tribes have been given the right to build casinos as a way of earning money to support their lifestyles.

Who were **Sitting Bull** and **Crazy Horse?**

Only in recent decades have the descendants of many Native Americans begun to tell the stories of their ancestors to people outside their tribes, thus helping modern-day students understand history from a Native American perspective. Archaeological digs continue to unearth artifacts that help reconstruct these people's ways of life, and some of their former settlements have been declared National Historic Sites. Pottery, blankets, and other Native American handiwork are in museum collections across the country, and some facilities have even recreated entire villages where you can walk among performers reenacting the day-to-day life of Native Americans.

You can learn more about all Native American tribes by visiting historical sites and museums. A list of these interesting places follows in the appendix.

APPENDIX

SITES AND MUSEUMS WHERE FAMILIES CAN LEARN MORE

Alabama

- **Birmingham Museum of Art.** The permanent collection includes 500 works of Native American art, and the museum offers tours, workshops and summer camps. www.artsbma.org
- **Florence Indian Mound and Museum.** Wawmanona, as it is known, is 42 feet high and believed to have been built around 500 CE. The site also houses an educational museum. www.flo-tour.org/indianmound.html
- **Russell Cave National Monument.** This site, maintained by the National Park Service, is toured with a ranger who demonstrates tools, weapons, and Native American ways of life. www.nps.gov/ruca/

Alaska

- **Alaska State Museum.** The permanent collection in Juneau includes galleries devoted to the Aleuts, Eskimos, Athabaskans, and Northwest Coast peoples. www.museums.state.ak.us
- **Anchorage Museum of History and Art.** The Kid's Corner program includes changing events geared toward hands-on learning. www.anchoragemuseum.org
- **Sheldon Jackson Museum.** This Sitka facility's programming includes demonstrations by native artists. www.museums.state.ak.us
- **Tongass Historical Museum and Totem Heritage Center.** Each of these sites near Ketchikan offers different programming, including native arts classes for children. www.city.ketchikan.ak.us/departments/museums/tongass.html

Arizona

- **Arizona State Museum.** Located in Tucson, the museum houses the largest collection of Southwest Indian pottery in the world. Items date back to the Hohokam and Mogollon periods. www.statemuseum.arizona.edu
- **Besh-Ba-Gowah Archaeological Park.** At this park, near Globe, you can walk through a 700-year-old pueblo and learn about its inhabitants at the site's museum. www.go-arizona.com/AZ/Besh-Ba-Gowah-Archaeological-Park
- **The Heard Museum.** This Phoenix institution strives to provide interactive exhibits that focus on Native American art and culture. Demonstrations and food, for instance, are sometimes part of the experience. www.heard.org
- **Pueblo Grande Museum.** This Phoenix museum is located at a 1,500-year-old Hohokam village ruin. Guided tours are available, and a museum and store are on site. www.ci.phoenix.az.us/PARKS/pueblo.html

Arkansas

- **Arkansas State University Museum.** The Native American gallery includes exhibits about tribes including the Caddo, Quapaw, Osage, Cherokee, Chickasaw, and Choctaw. http://museum.astate.edu
- **Hampson Archaeological Museum State Park.** This Northeast Arkansas site houses exhibits and artifacts from the people who lived there between 1400 and 1650 CE. www.arkansasstateparks.com

California

- **Antelope Valley Indian Research Museum.** Near Lancaster, this museum has developed grade-appropriate tours that explore more than 12,000 years of history. www.avim.parks.ca.gov
- **The Bowers Museum.** "First Californians" is part of the permanent collection. The exhibit includes many California tribes, but focuses on coastal people. A teaching resource guide is available in the gift shop. www.bowers.org
- **Indian Grinding Rock State Historic Park.** Northeast of Stockton, this park includes a museum and a reconstructed Miwok village. Local Native Americans hold ceremonies here annually, including an annual Acorn Harvest Thanksgiving each September. www.parks.ca.gov

Colorado

- **Denver Art Museum.** The American Indian collection includes more than 16,000 art objects and represents more than 100 tribes from across the United States and Canada. Kid's Corner activities are available daily. www.denverartmuseum.org
- **Denver Museum of Nature and Science.** The North American Indian Cultures exhibit was created with the theme "We are all different, we are all the same." It includes a reconstructed snow house, Northwest Coast clan house, Navajo hogan, and Cheyenne teepee. www.dmns.org
- **Ute Indian Museum.** Located near Montrose, this is one of the only U.S. museums devoted solely to the history of one tribe. The building is on a farm once owned by an Ute leader. www.visitmontrose.net/indian_museum.htm

Connecticut

- **Mashantucket Pequot Museum and Research Center.** Life-size dioramas and live exhibits are part of the learning experience at this facility in Mashantucket. There are also two libraries, one designed for children. www.pequotmuseum.org
- **Peabody Museum of Natural History.** This museum, on the Yale University Campus, includes a Hall of Native American Cultures with items from tribes including the Blackfoot, Apache, Sioux, Cheyenne, Crow, Navaho, Zuni, Hopi, and Pima. www.peabody.yale.edu
- **Tantaquidgeon Indian Museum.** This one-room museum was built by a Mohegan family in the 1930s. It's located in Uncasville, near the Mohegan Sun casino and resort. www.nationaltrust.org

Delaware

- **Delaware Archaeology Museum.** An overview of Delaware's Native American history is a central part of the exhibits at this museum, which is dedicated to examining the process of archaeology. The museum is in Dover. www.destatemuseums.org

District of Columbia

- **National Museum of Natural History.** This museum is part of the Smithsonian Institution and has many exhibitions and programs about the first Americans. www.mnh.si.edu

Florida

- **Ah-Ta-Thi-Ki Seminole Museum.** The name of this museum means "to learn," which you can do throughout the regular exhibits and a living Seminole village. www.seminoletribe.com/museum

- **Indian Temple Mound Museum.** Fort Walton Beach is home to this 6,000-artifact institution, which includes what is perhaps the largest prehistoric earthwork built on the Gulf Coast. www.fwb.org

Georgia

- **Chieftains Museum and Major Ridge Home.** This National Historic Landmark was once the home of early 1800s Cherokee leader Major Ridge. It is a site on the Trail of Tears National Historic Trail. www.chieftainsmuseum.org/

Idaho

- **Nez Perce National Historical Park.** This park comprises 38 sites in Idaho, Oregon, Washington, and Montana that commemorate the stories of the Nez Perce people. Scavenger hunts and walking tours are among the activities that families can enjoy together. www.nps.gov/nepe/
- **Shoshone-Bannock Indian Festival.** Held the second weekend of August, this annual event draws tribes from around the United States. Dancing, rodeo, arts, and crafts are among the many sights and activities. www.shoshonebannocktribes.com/festival.html

Illinois

- **Dickson Mounds Museum.** Located in west-central Illinois, this on-site archaeological museum has interpretive exhibits, hands-on activities and special events year-round. www.museum.state.il.us/ismsites/dickson/
- **Mitchell Museum of the American Indian.** This museum, at Kendall College in Evanston, has nearly 10,000 objects and more than 5,000 books about Native American history and culture. www.mitchellmuseum.org
- **Schingoethe Center for Native American Cultures at Aurora University.** More than 6,000 pieces are part of the collection here, and powwows are held annually. www.aurora.edu/museum/

Indiana

- **Eiteljorg Museum of American Indians and Western Art.** Located in Indianapolis, this museum houses traditional and modern art. It even has a café that serves Native American–inspired cuisine. www.eiteljorg.org
- **Mathers Museum of World Cultures.** More than 8,000 objects, many from Eskimos, Pawnees, Seminoles, and Navajos, fill the collection at this Bloomington institution. Educational services area available for children of all ages. www.indiana.edu/~mathers/
- **Mounds State Park.** About 70 miles east of Anderson, this park features 10 earthen works built by the Adena-Hopewell tribe. The largest was believed to have been built in 160 BCE for religious ceremonies. www.in.gov/dnr/parklake/properties/park_mounds.html

Iowa

- **Effigy Mounds National Monument.** This northeast Iowa site includes several types of mounds, including animal effigy, bird effigy, and conical and linear types. www.nps.gov/efmo/pphtml/nature.html
- **Putnam Museum.** Based in Davenport, this museum's permanent "River, Prairie and People" exhibit includes a timeline of the region's history starting with Native American people. www.putnam.org

Kansas

- **Kansas Museum of History.** Native American history is a major theme at this museum, whose exhibits include arrowheads, pottery, a Cheyenne war lance, a towering teepee, a 5,000-year-old human effigy head, and more. www.kshs.org

➤ **Native American Heritage Museum.** This museum near Highland contains interactive exhibits about the Great Lakes tribes that were forced to move to Kansas in the 1800s. www.kshs.org

➤ **Pawnee Indian Village Museum.** Near the town of Republic, this museum introduces you to an 1820s earth lodge that once housed some of the 2,000 Pawnees who lived in the village. The remains of other houses are on the grounds, as well. www.kshs.org

Kentucky

➤ **Speed Art Museum.** Based in Louisville, the state's oldest and largest art museum has a Native American collection that includes artifacts from tribes including the Sioux, Cheyenne, Arapaho, Kiowa, and Crow. www.speedmuseum.org

➤ **Wickliffe Mounds State Historic Site.** This archaeological site overlooking the Mississippi River includes a tourist operation known as the Ancient Buried City. A museum showcases items that have been excavated from the site in recent decades. http://parks.ky.gov/statehistoricsites/wm/

Louisiana

➤ **Louisiana State Exhibit Museum.** This Shreveport museum houses an excellent collection of Caddo, Coushatta, Choctaw, and Chitimacha Indian artifacts. www.sec.state.la.us/museums/shreve/shreve-index.htm

➤ **Snyder Memorial Museum and Creative Arts Center.** Originally a private home, this 1929 dwelling in Bastrop has been converted into a museum that contains items from the Poverty Point Indian mounds and ceramics from Mexican tribes. (318) 281-8760

➤ **Tunica-Biloxi Regional Indian Center and Museum.** This Marksville institution holds a collection of Indian/ European artifacts from the state's Colonial period. (318) 253-0213

Maine

➤ **Abbe Museum.** "Celebrating Maine's Native American Heritage," this Bar Harbor institution houses more than 50,000 objects representing 10,000 years of culture and history. www.abbemuseum.org

➤ **Penobscot Nation Museum.** This Indian island museum showcases historical art as well as contemporary Wabanaki works such as paintings, wood carvings, and basketry. www.penobscotnation.org/museum/indox.htm

Maryland

➤ **Piscataway Indian Museum.** This museum contains historical and contemporary artifacts from the Eastern Woodlands, Plains, Northwest, and Southwest. A trading post is nearby for purchasing Native American arts, crafts, and more. www.piscatawayindians.org/museum

Massachusetts

➤ **Natick Historical Society and Museum.** Housed on the lower level of the Bacon Free Library building in South Natick, the museum collection includes artifacts of Archaic, Woodland, and Christian Indian cultures. www.natickhistory.com

➤ **Peabody Museum of Archaeology and Ethnology.** This museum at Harvard University is quite strong in archeological pieces and has an exhibit running through December 2006 titled "From Nation to Nation: Examining Lewis & Clark's Indian Collection." www.peabody.harvard.edu

➤ **Peabody Essex Museum.** Located in Salem, this museum's Native American collection includes thousands of historic works. www.pem.org

➤ **Plimoth Plantation.** This living history experience in Plymouth allows you to walk through an early pilgrim settlement and its contemporary Native American village. "Pilgrims" and "Native Americans" go about their daily lives, interacting with visitors along the way. www.plimoth.org

Michigan

- **The Detroit Institute of Arts.** An expansion is under way in this museum's Indigenous American Art Collection, which is scheduled to move into a gallery triple its current size in 2007. www.dia.org
- **Norton Mounds.** Located south of Grand Rapids, this complex of Hopewell earth works are believed to be 2,000 years old. It is one of the best-preserved Hopewell sites in the region. www.grmuseum.org/nortonmounds/index.shtml
- **Public Museum of Grand Rapids.** Nearly 100 Anishinabe people helped to create the exhibition at this museum that tells the story of their history. The exhibit is part of one of the largest collections relating to Native American cultures in the state. www.grmuseum.org

Minnesota

- **Mille Lacs Indian Museum.** Located on Lake Mille Lacs about 12 miles north of Onamia, this museum tells the history of the Mille Lacs band of Ojibwe Native Americans. A crafts room offers demonstrations of traditional cooking, birch-bark basketry, and beadwork. www.mnhs.org/places/sites/mlim/index.html
- **North West Company Fur Post.** A recreated Ojibwe settlement is part of the educational experience at this Pine City institution, where costumed guides lead the way. www.mnhs.org/places/sites/nwcfp/
- **Science Museum of Minnesota.** Among the collections at this St. Paul museum are artifacts from tribes including the Dakota, Ojibwe, Sauk, Fox, Winnebago, and Ottawa. The Warren Basketry Collection includes 150 examples of Native American basketry from the western Great Lakes region. www.smm.org

Mississippi

- **The Grand Village of the Natchez Indians.** This 128-acre site in the town of Natchez includes a museum, a reconstructed Natchez house, and three ceremonial mounds. www.mdah.state.ms.us/hprop/gvni.html
- **Mississippi Crafts Center.** A mile north of Jackson, this facility offers crafts demonstrations, classes, and festivals. Items for sale include cane basket designs by members of the Choctaw tribe, as well as pottery, woven items, quilts, and jewelry. (601) 856-7546

Missouri

- **Fort Osage.** Lewis and Clark discovered this site in the early 1800s and noted its excellent characteristics as the home for a future fort. It sits in the modern-day town of Sibley and is now a stop on the 8,000-mile-long Lewis and Clark Historic National Trail. You can learn about the Osage people here, and much more. www.historicfortosage.com
- **Graham Cave State Park.** Located in Montgomery City, this 360-acre state park includes a cave that once held artifacts from the Archaic period. Visitors can enter the cave and learn about the discoveries made by University of Missouri archaeologists. www.mostateparks.com/grahamcave.htm
- **Nelson-Atkins Museum of Art.** This Kansas City institution has a collection of Plains and Southwest Native American artworks including Navajo blankets, Pueblo pottery, and California basketry. Classes and events are scheduled regularly for adults and children alike. www.nelson-atkins.org

Montana

- **Flathead Indian Museum and Trading Post.** If you want to examine and perhaps even purchase Native American crafts, art, and artifacts, this St. Ignatius spot is for you. There is also a wildlife exhibit on site. http://indiannations.visitmt.com

- **Lodgepole Gallery and Tipi Village.** Located in Browning, this traditional Blackfoot teepee camp offers overnight stays in teepees along with traditional food, horse demonstrations, and arts and crafts. Cultural history tours can also be arranged. http://indiannations.visitmt.com
- **The People's Center.** This Pablo cultural center, in the heart of the Flathead Indian Reservation, includes an exhibit gallery, educational programs, and interpretive tours that focus on Native American heritage and natural history. http://indiannations.visitmt.com

Nebraska

- **Fort Robinson Museum.** Exhibits at this Crawford museum trace its history from the mid-1800s, including how it once hosted the great Chief Crazy Horse. A number of nineteenth-century Sioux objects are on display, as well. www.nebraskahistory.org/sites/fortrob/
- **John G. Neihardt State Historical Site.** Neihardt, Nebraska's poet laureate, is best known as the author of Black Elk Speaks, the biography of the visionary Oglala Lakota holy man. The site contains the study where he wrote as well as a Sacred Hoop Prayer Garden planted under his direction. Conferences and events are held at the site annually. www.nebraskahistory.org/sites/neihardt/
- **Museum of the Fur Trade.** Three miles east of Chadron, this museum has three galleries that explore the history of the fur trade, including the participation of Plains and Woodland Indians. It sits on the grounds of an original trading post. www.furtrade.org/

Nevada

- **Lost City Museum.** This Overton institution was built to house Anasazi artifacts that were excavated from the Pueblo Grande de Nevada. Special public programs are held throughout the year by the state park service, which oversees the site. http://dmla.clan.lib.nv.us/docs/museums/lost/lostcity.htm
- **Old Logandale School.** This Logandale institution has been restored to serve as a cultural center that includes an art gallery, a reference library, and more. www.olshacs.org
- **Stewart Indian Museum.** Located in Carson City, this museum was once the site of the Stewart Indian School. Today, it includes a trading post with collectibles including rugs, silver jewelry, and art. www.tahoenevada.com

New Hampshire

- **America's Stonehenge.** This North Salem site is home to a maze of manmade chambers, walls, and ceremonial meeting places that may have been built by Native Americans as many as 4,000 years ago. www.stonehengeusa.com
- **Mount Kearsarge Indian Museum.** Based in Warner, this museum offers guided tours, more than a thousand artifacts, and a Medicine Woods Nature Trail that is planted with many of the plants, trees, and herbs that Native Americans used to create food, medicine, and tools. www.indianmuseum.org

New Jersey

- **Hopewell Museum.** This museum, based in the town of Hopewell, showcases Native American crafts including early tools and farm implements. Admission is free. (609) 466-0103
- **Lake Hopatcong Historical Museum.** Located in the town of Landing, this museum traces the lake's history back to the time when the Lenape tribe lived along its shores. Tours are available. www.hopatcong.org/museum

New Mexico

- **Indian Pueblo Cultural Center.** This Albuquerque institution showcases the history and accomplishments of the Pueblo people from pre-Columbian days to the present. More than 200,000 people visit each year. www.indianpueblo.org

- **Roswell Museum and Art Center.** Based in the town of Roswell, this museum includes a collection of nearly 2,000 artifacts including Native American finds. There is also a planetarium on site. www.roswellmuseum.org
- **Wheelwright Museum of the American Indian.** Located in Santa Fe, this museum has changing exhibits that highlight contemporary and traditional Native American art, with a focus on the Southwest tribes. The trading post has many goodies for sale, as well. www.wheelwright.org
- **Zuni Pueblo.** This pueblo is believed to have been the first that Spanish explorers visited in the 1500s. Located about 150 miles west of Albuquerque, the pueblo includes restaurants, recreation, and nearly a dozen different shops. www.ashiwi.net

New York

- **American Museum of Natural History.** This Manhattan institution has permanent exhibitions including the Hall of Northwest Coast Indians and the Hall of Eastern Woodlands and Plains Indians. Tools on display include cooking utensils, weapons, jewelry, and more. www.amnh.org
- **Iroquois Indian Museum.** Located in Howes Cave, west of Schenectady between the Adirondacks and the Catskills, this facility includes a separate children's museum with hands-on crafts and games. Stone tools are a key feature of the museum's archaeology game. www.iroquoismuseum.org
- **National Museum of the American Indian.** Also in Manhattan, this museum hosts exhibitions and events in conjunction with its sister museum in Washington, D.C. Student and family programs are available. www.nmai.si.edu

North Carolina

- **Frisco Native American Museum & Natural History Center.** This museum is on Hatteras Island in the Outer Banks and includes exhibits, nature trails, and an annual powwow that usually is held in early spring. http://nativeamericanmuseum.org
- **Museum of the Native American Resource Center.** Located in Pembroke, this museum has collections that focus on art, crafts, music, literature, history, and more. It also includes an interesting exhibit about a mid-1950s battle against the Ku Klux Klan. www.uncp.edu/nativemuseum
- **Rankin Museum of American and Natural History.** This Ellerbe facility emphasizes the history and culture of early American life, including special exhibits dedicated to tribes from the Southeast, Plains, Northwest Coast, Arctic, and Amazon. www.rankinmuseum.com

North Dakota

- **Fort Totten State Historic Site.** This state historic site is in Bismarck. It once served as a Native American boarding school, health-care facility, and reservation school. Today, it houses a museum, an interpretive center, and more. www.state.nd.us/hist/totten/totten.htm
- **On-A-Slant Mandan Village.** Part of the Fort Abraham Lincoln foundation in the town of Mandan, this village includes five reconstructed earth lodges that you can tour with a guide who will explain the local Native American history. www.fortlincoln.com
- **Three Tribes Museum.** Located in New Town, this museum includes displays, artifacts, and pictures relating to the history of the Mandan, Hidatsa, and Arikara tribes. www.lewisandclarktrail.com

Ohio

- **Flint Ridge.** Located in Glenford, this ridge contains quarry pits where Native Americans went to get flint for tools, weapons, and trade. The site now includes a museum, a shop, and a picnic area. www.ohiohistory.org/places/flint
- **Fort Ancient Museum.** Located in Oregomia, this archaeological site includes a Hopewell earthwork that is part of a National Historic Site. The grounds also include a museum, hiking trails, and picnicking areas. (513) 932-4421

→ **Serpent Mound State Memorial.** This national historical landmark is near Locust Grove and is the largest serpent effigy in all of North America. www.ohiohistory.org/places/serpent/

Oklahoma

→ **Ataloa Lodge Museum.** The director of this museum, which is at Bacone College in Muskogee, is a citizen of the Muscogee/Creek nation. He is a master flute maker who often plays at the request of guests. www.bacone.edu/ataloa

→ **Cherokee National Museum.** Located in Talequah, includes a museum, an ancient village, and a rural village. It also houses the official archives of the Cherokee Nation and changing exhibits about the tribe's history. www.powersource.com/heritage/museum.html

→ **Indian City USA.** This Anadarko institution includes seven replicas of Native American villages, a gift shop including handmade, authentic works, a museum, a campground, and a 140-acre exotic game preserve featuring buffalo, deer, wild turkeys, and more. www.indiancityusa.com

Oregon

→ **Favell Museum.** Located in Klamath Falls, this well-regarded museum features Western art and Native American artifacts. You'll be able to see sculptures, wood carvings, arrowheads, clothing, beadwork, tools, and more. www.favellmuseum.org

→ **Heritage Museum.** Housed in a neoclassical building in Astoria, this museum's displays include Native American artifacts as well as information about early immigrants and settlers. www.oldoregon.com.

→ **Wallowa Nez Perce Interpretive Center.** This National Historic Park site hosts a three-day pow-wow and celebration each summer. It includes a friendship feast, speeches, songs, and prayer. www.wallowanezperce.com.

Pennsylvania

→ **Carnegie Museum of Natural History.** The Alcoa Foundation Hall of Native Americans at this Pittsburgh institution focuses on the Tlingit of the Northwest Coast, the Hopi of the Southwest, the Lakota of the Plains, and the Iroquois of the Northeast. www.carnegiemnh.org

→ **Lenni Lenape Historical Society and Museum of Indian Culture.** Founded in 1980, this eighteenth-century farmhouse in Allentown includes various exhibits as well as a library and resource center. www.lenape.org

→ **Pocono Indian Museum.** Located in Bushkill, this is the only museum in northeastern Pennsylvania dedicated to the history of the Delaware Indian. Displays include artifacts, weapons, and tools. www.poconoindianmuseum.com

Rhode Island

→ **Haffenreffer Museum of Anthropology.** Based at Brown University in Bristol, this museum has exhibits that feature Native American skin and wooden kayaks and canoes, Hopi dolls, and more. www.brown.edu

→ **Tomaquag Indian Memorial Museum.** This Exeter museum has large collections of ash splint baskets and corn husk dolls. It hosts classes, celebrations, and other events year-round. www.tomaquagmuseum.com

South Dakota

→ **Crazy Horse Memorial.** Seventeen miles southwest of Mount Rushmore, this memorial includes the Indian Museum of North America, the Native American Cultural Center, a sculptor's studio, and more. During the summer months, many artists visit here to create new works and visit with the public. www.crazyhorse.org

➡ **Journey Museum.** Based in Rapid City, this institution includes a Sioux Indian Museum that tells the story of the Lakota nation. There is even a storyteller who will recount the tales and traditions of the Lakota culture. www.journeymuseum.org

➡ **South Dakota Art Museum.** Located at South Dakota State University, this museum includes thousands of pieces of Native American artifacts and art. The exhibits in its seven galleries are presented on a rotating basis. www3.sdstate.edu/Administration/SouthDakotaArtMuseum

Tennessee

➡ **Chucalissa Museum.** Based in Memphis, this museum and reconstructed village are operated by the Department of Anthropology at the University of Memphis. It is a National Historic Landmark. http://cas.memphis.edu/chucalissa/

➡ **Frank H. McClung Museum.** One of the permanent exhibits at this University of Tennessee museum in Knoxville is "Archaeology and the Native Peoples of Tennessee." It includes findings from more than 65 years of research by university archaeologists. http://mcclungmuseum.utk.edu/

➡ **Sequoyah Birthplace Museum.** Located in Vonore, this facility celebrates the Cherokee named Sequoyah who invented a writing system that later was used throughout the Cherokee Nation and the United States. It is a stop on the Trail of Tears National Historic Trail. www.sequoyahmuseum.org

Texas

➡ **Cowboy Museum.** This museum is located right across from the Alamo in San Antonio. It displays artifacts from the Old West and, in particular, the 1870s. (210) 229-1257

➡ **Fort Concho.** A National Historic Landmark, this San Angelo site includes 23 original and restored structures from the outpost that was built on the Concho River in 1867. www.fortconcho.com

➡ **Houston Museum of Natural Science.** One of the permanent exhibits at this institution is the John P. McGovern Hall of the Americas. It includes artifacts, arts, and crafts representing more than 50 Native American cultures from Alaska to Peru. www.hmns.mus.tx.us

➡ **Panhandle-Plains Historical Museum.** This Houston institution is billed as the largest history museum in Texas. It houses a permanent exhibit titled "People of the Plains" that traces 14,000 years of human existence across the Southern Great Plains region. www.panhandleplains.org

Utah

➡ **Anasazi State Park Museum.** Located in Boulder, this ancient village was one of the largest Anasazi communities west of the Colorado River, housing as many as 200 people. You can explore the site, as well as enjoy educational exhibits at the nearby museum. www.stateparks.utah.gov/park_pages/anasazi.htm

➡ **College of Eastern Utah Prehistoric Museum.** This Price City museum's Hall of Man includes an exhibit about the culture of the Ute Native Americans, who spoke Shoshone and from whose name the state got its moniker. http://museum.ceu.edu/default.htm

➡ **Museum of Peoples and Cultures.** Based at Brigham Young University in Provo, this teaching museum includes rotating exhibits that focus on different Native American peoples, and more. http://fhss.byu.edu/anthro/mopc/main.htm

Virginia

➡ **Jamestown Rediscovery.** This facility traces the history of the first permanent English colony of the Americas. You can tour the excavation site from the 1600s, visit the Old Town on a guided tour, and much more. www.apva.org/jr.html

➤ **Jamestown Settlement.** A living history museum focusing on the relationship between the Powhatan Indians and the European and African immigrants. Open year-round. www.historyisfun.org

➤ **Virginia Museum of Natural History.** Located in Martinsville, this child-friendly institution includes rotating exhibits that, among other things, focus on the Lakota Native Americans. During summer Fridays, special activities are planned for families to enjoy together. www.vmnh.net

Washington

➤ **Burke Museum of Natural History and Culture.** This University of Washington museum, based in Seattle, includes rotating exhibits about the history, culture, and crafts of Native American people. Tours are available for children's groups during summertime. www.washington.edu/burkemuseum/

➤ **Lewis and Clark Interpretive Center.** Located at Cape Disappointment State Park, about two miles southwest of Ilwaco, this cliff-top institute uses timeline murals to trace the journey of the Lewis and Clark expedition. A shop and observation desk is also on site. www.parks.wa.gov/lewisandclark/lcinterpctr.asp

➤ **Makah Cultural and Research Center.** Open from Memorial Day through mid-September, this facility on Neah Bay includes artifacts from the Makah people. The exhibits include a full-size replica long house, dugout canoes, and more. www.makah.com

➤ **Northwest Museum of Arts and Culture.** This Spokane institution's permanent collection includes one of the nation's finest groupings of Plateau Native American artifacts. Works of living Native American artists also are highlighted. www.northwestmuseum.org

West Virginia

➤ **Pocahontas County Historical Museum.** Located in Marlinton, this museum is open only during the summer and displays exhibits relating to the history of the local people. (304) 799-6659

➤ **Washington's Lands Museum and Sayre Log House.** This Ravenswood facility is inside an old log house on the Ohio River. It includes a few Native American artifacts, along with many tools and furniture used by the area's early settlers. www.museumsofwv.org

Wisconsin

➤ **Aztalan State Park.** Located in Lake Mills, this park's archaeological site showcases an ancient Middle-Mississippian village and ceremonial complex. You can walk along the reconstructed mounds or visit the nearby church. Picnicking, hiking, and other park activities are also available. www.dnr.state.wi.us/org/land/parks/specific/aztalan/

➤ **Milwaukee Public Museum.** Among the permanent collections at this institution is "North American Indians and North American Ecology," which includes a powwow grand entry scene featuring 37 life-size figures that move on a large turntable, as if dancing. Nearby exhibits trace the history of the region's tribes. www.mpm.edu

Wyoming

➤ **Buffalo Bill Historical Center.** This Cody facility includes a Plains Indians museum that highlights, among other things, the Lakota, Crow, Arapaho, Shoshone, and Cheyenne tribes. A powwow is held each June, with dancers from across North America competing for prizes. www.bbhc.org

➤ **Fort Laramie National Historic Site.** Originally a fur trading post, this frontier outpost closed in 1890 but continues to offer a glimpse into life at the time when the Cheyenne and Arapaho met white settlers for the first time. Self-guided audio tours are available. www.nps.gov/fola/

➤ **Museum of the Mountain Man.** Located in Pinedale, this facility's permanent exhibits include Native American clothes and artifacts. You'll also learn a lot here about the importance of the western fur trade. www.museumofthemountainman.com/

GLOSSARY

A

adobe: sun-dried brick, or the clay from which these bricks are made

adze: an ax-like tool for trimming and smoothing wood

anadromous: a fish that returns from the sea to the river it was born in to breed

Anasazi: the group of Native Americans who conquered the Mogollons and built great structures out of adobe; their name means "ancient people" in the Hopi language

aqueduct: a large pipe or conduit made for bringing water from a distant source

archaeology: the scientific study of human life and culture of the past, by excavation of ancient cities and artifacts

Arctic: the region around the North Pole, including the Arctic Ocean and the surrounding land north of 70 degrees latitude

astronomy: the science of the universe in which the stars, planets, etc. are studied

atlatl: a thick, hollowed-out stick or bone used as a spear-throwing tool

Aztec: the people who lived in present-day Mexico and had an advanced civilization before their conquest by Cortes in 1519

B

baby frame: a wooden board that mothers strapped their babies into; it was hung from a hook to keep babies safely out of the way during chore times

bareback: riding a horse without a saddle

Battle of Little Bighorn: also known as Custer's Last Stand; a battle fought in 1876 between U.S. Lieutenant Colonel George Armstrong Custer and thousands of Native Americans led by Chiefs Crazy Horse and Sitting Bull

Beringia: an exposed mass of land that scientists believe once connected Asia and the Americas

biface tool: a rock or bone tool having two sides chipped for use

bullboat: a round boat made from a frame of willow branches covered in buffalo hide

C

carbon-14 testing: a scientific method for determining an artifact's age based on the amount of carbon 14 element it still contains

chinampas: floating gardens used by the Aztecs in the city of Tenochtitlán

chisel: a hand tool with a sharp, often wedge-shaped, blade for cutting or shaping wood and stone

cistern: a large receptacle for storing water

climate shift: a major change in regional temperature and weather, such as between the Ice Age and the present

Clovis culture: the lifestyle of Native Americans who hunted using spear points found at an archaeological site near Clovis, New Mexico

corn silk: the long, silky fibers that hang out of a corn husk; sometimes used to make doll hair for Native American children

D

dibble: a digging stick used by Hopi farmers

dip net: a bag of netting suspended from a Y- or V-shaped wooden frame; used for fishing

E

Eskimo: a derogatory nickname meaning "eaters of raw meat," given to the northernmost Native Americans by the Algonquian tribes from the south

extinct: no longer in existence

F

food chain: a sequence of organisms in a community in which each member feeds on the one below it

G

gouge: a chisel with a curved, hollowed blade, for cutting grooves or holes in wood

H

hieroglyphic: a system of writing in which a picture or symbol representing a word or syllable is used instead of letters

Hohokam: the "Vanished Ones" who dominated the Southwest for 2,000 years, starting around 400 BCE and lasting until about 1500 CE

I

igloo: a house or hut, usually dome-shaped, built of blocks of packed snow

Indian Removal Act: legislation passed in 1830 and signed into law by President Andrew Jackson stating that all Native Americans living east of the Mississippi River had to move west, into present-day Oklahoma

Inuit: the name the northernmost Native Americans who lived in the Arctic chose for themselves, meaning "The People"

irrigation: the process of supplying crops with water by means of ditches or artificial channels, or by sprinklers

K

kashim: a ceremony house used by Inuit men, built in the center of a group of sod dwellings

kiva: a large room used for religious and other purposes by the Hopi

L

lattice: an openwork structure of crossed strips or bars of wood, metal, or other material, used as a screen or support

leister: a fish spear, usually with three prongs

literate, literacy: the ability to read and write

longhouse: the traditional sleeping building of the Iroquois, as much as 150 feet long with curtained "booths" that families slept in

M

magnetite: a type of iron ore in which you can sometimes see your reflection

maize: a type of corn

Manifest Destiny: the nineteenth-century idea that the continued territorial expansion of the United States was inevitable

Maya: a tribe with a highly developed civilization that dominated the Yucatan, Belize, and northern Guatemala

mesa: a widespread flat area at high elevation with one or more cliff-like sides

Mesoamerica: the region that includes parts of Mexico and Central America, inhabited by various Native American civilizations

migrate: to move from one place to another, as in leaving one's country and settling in another; to move from one region to another with the change in seasons

moccasin: a shoe made of soft, flexible leather or animal skin

Mogollon: the hunting and gathering civilization that existed in the Rocky Mountain region from about 300 BCE until about 1300 CE

N

nugluktaq: an Inuit game played by poking sticks into a twirling spool

P

Papago: close allies of the Pima who lived in and around Arizona—they call themselves Tohono O'Odhan

pigment: any coloring matter found in nature

Pima: expert makers of watertight baskets who lived near the Gila River in Arizona

potlatch: a ceremony, sometimes lasting for several days, at which a host lavishes gifts upon his guests

powwow: a gathering of Native Americans for the purpose of discussing common issues, celebrating wartime success, curing disease, and so forth

Pueblo Revolution: a Native American uprising that occurred in 1680 in present-day New Mexico; led by a medicine man named Popé, the fighting claimed the lives of about 400 Spanish settlers

pueblo: a type of communal village consisting of one or more flat-roofed structures of stone or adobe, arranged in terraces and housing a number of families

Q

Quetzalcoatl: the Feathered Serpent, one of the main gods of all Mesoamerican civilizations
quinzy: a snow cave

R

redd: a spawning area of trout or salmon
relic: item that people from a previous time period used in a given place
reservation: public land set aside for a special use, such as the relocation of Native Americans in the 1800s
roe: fish eggs

S

sapling: a young tree
silo: an airtight pit or tower in which food can be preserved
snare: an overhead net attached to a ground-level trigger, designed to entangle animals
spawn: to produce or deposit eggs, sperm, or young
species: a distinct population of similar organisms that usually interbreed only among themselves
stelae: upright stone slabs or pillars engraved with inscriptions or designs and used as monuments and grave markers

T

talud-tablero: a building technique with sloped walls covered with decorative panels
Tenochtitlán: an Aztec city built on Lake Texcoco that eventually housed about 200,000 people
Teotihuacán: a city whose name means "Abode of the Gods," populated by as many as 200,000 Aztecs and spanning about eight square miles
tepee: a cone-shaped tent of animal skins or bark

Thanksgiving: a name given to the feast that the Native Americans and pilgrims shared after the harvest of 1621
thatch: straw, leaves, or any similar material used for making a roof
Tikal: a city whose name means "Place of Voices," built in present-day Guatemala around 200 BCE and spanning 23 square miles; it housed as many as 100,000 to 200,000 Maya people
tomahawk: a war club on a wooden stick—after the Europeans came to the Americas and introduced metal, a spiked metal ball was often affixed to the top
totem: an emblem of a family or clan, often a reminder of its ancestry; usually a carved or painted representation of such an object
totem pole: a pole or post carved and painted with totems; often erected in front of Native American dwellings
Trail of Tears: path of a thousand miles walked by Cherokees in 1838 when they were forced from their homelands and sent to live on reservations in present-day Oklahoma
transient: temporary, staying only a short time
travois: a sled consisting of a net or platform dragged along the ground on two poles that are pulled by a horse or dog
treaty: a formal agreement between two parties relating to peace, alliance, trade, and/or property

U

uniface tool: a rock or bone tool having one side chipped for use

W

Wampanoag: Native Americans encountered by the *Mayflower* Pilgrims; from the Algonquian words *wampa*, meaning "dawn," and *noag*, meaning "people"
wampum: seashells strung together into long belts that could be used to convey messages or as currency
weir: a fence or obstruction built in a river or stream to divert water or catch fish

INDEX

A

Activities,
  Algonquian Art, 32
  Archaeological Site, 8, 9
  Archaic Toolkit, 20
  Face Painting, 24
  Family Totem Pole, 86
  Hieroglyphics, 64
  Ice Age, 6
  Irrigation, 60, 61
  Miniature Bullboat, 49
  Names from History, 103
  Navajo Dry Painting, 72
  Navajo Jewelry, 74
  Nugluktaq, 93
  Quinzy, 90, 91
  Rattle, 47
  Speak Algonquian, 30
  War Bonnet, 50, 51
  X-ray Art, 83
adobe, 57, 58, 61
Adena, 21, 22
adzes, 30, 31
Alabama, 38
Alaska, 4
Algonquian, iv, vi, 27, 29–36, 38, 88
Älsé, vi, 76
Anasazi, 23, 26, 57–63, 69
Ankawoo, 84
Apache, vi, 71, 73
Appalachian Mountains, 37, 38
archaeology, archaeologist 3, 8, 9, 11, 13, 15, 19 28, 33, 62, 106
Archaic Period, 17–21
Arctic, Arctic Ocean, vi, 2, 4, 5, 26, 28, 87–96
Arizona, 25, 58, 69, 71
art, 15, 16, 22, 23, 32, 47, 50, 72, 83. *See also* jewelry.
Asia, 4, 5, 7, 88

Atlantic Ocean, 4, 7, 19, 37
atlatl, 21, 22
Aztec, iv, vi, 62, 63, 65–68

B

baby frame, 30, 31
baskets, vi, 14, 26, 58, 68, 69
Battle of Little Bighorn, 104, 105
Beringia, Bering Strait, 3–5, 7, 13
biface tool, 14, 16
books, iv, 58, 67
bows, bow and arrow, 21, 30
buffalo, vi, 45–50, 52, 71, 100
bullboats, vi, 48, 49, 52
burial grounds, mounds, 19, 21

C

calendar, 2, 58, 67
California, v, 7
Canada, 45
canoe, 30, 31, 79, 84
carbon-14 testing, 11–13, 21
Carolinas, the, v, 37, 38, 44
Catawba, vi, 37, 42–44
Cayuga, vi, 36
ceremonies. *See* religion.
Cherokee Phoenix and Indian Advocate, The, iv, 41
Cherokee, iv–vi, 2, 38–44, 102
Cheyenne, vi, 45–56, 105
Chickasaw, 42, 102
Chile, 13
chinampas, 66–68
Chinook, vi, 76, 84
chisel, 31
Choctaw, 42, 102
cloth, clothing, 8, 10, 12, 14, 21, 23, 35, 47, 58, 100, 106
Clovis culture, 12, 13, 16
colonies, colonists, iv, 36, 40, 41, 50, 56, 73, 97–102, 105

Colorado, 25, 8, 59, 71
Columbus, Christopher, 26, 98
Comanche, vi, 45–56
Connecticut, 27
Coos, vi, 76
Coquille, vi, 76
corn. *See* maize.
Cortez, Hernando, iv, 68
Crazy Horse, 97, 105, 106
Creek, vi, 37, 42–44, 102
crops. *See* farming.
Custer, George Armstrong, 104, 105

D

Dakotas, the, 45, 54
dance, 16. *See also* music.
De Soto, Hernando, 26
Delaware, 27
dibble, 70
dogs, 46, 52, 95, 96
duma, 70

E

Europe, Europeans, 4, 7, 21, 26, 30, 34, 41, 50, 56, 71, 73, 97–100, 105
explorers, iv, 21, 26, 30, 34, 98
extinction, 10, 17, 18, 101

F

farming, vi, 11, 17, 18, 21, 31, 33, 38, 43, 57, 60, 68, 69, 99
fish, fishing, vi, 4, 10, 15, 26, 27, 31, 38, 48, 75–81, 83
Five Nations, the, 36
Florida, iv, 44, 102
food. *See* buffalo, farming, fishing, hunting, maize, seals, spears, whales.
Formative Period, 17–26
Fort Sumner, v, 102

BIBLIOGRAPHY

Books

Dillehay, Thomas D., *The Settlement of the Americas*, Perseus/Basic Books, 2000

Maxswell, James A., *America's Fascinating Indian Heritage*, Reader's Digest Books, 1978

Nies, Judith, *Native American History: A Chronology of a Culture's Vast Achievements and Their Links to World Events*, Ballantine Books, 1996

Pritzker, Barry M., *A Native American Encyclopedia: History, Culture and Peoples*, Oxford University Press, 2000

Stuart, George E., *Ancient Pioneers: The First Americans*, National Geographic Society, 2001

Web Sites

www.500nations.com
www.ccppcrafts.com
www.choctaw.org
www.ftmcdowell.org
www.hopi.nsn.us

www.mohegan.nsn.us
www.narragensett-tribe.org
www.navajo.org
www.notoweega.org
www.pequotmuseum.org

www.rednation.org
www.seminoletribe.com
www.standingrock.org
www.wmat.nsn.us